Pilgrim Ways

Pilgrim Ways

A holiday guide to the
Christian 'Holy Places'
of Britain and Ireland

DAVID MARSHALL

AUTUMN

HOUSE

COVER PHOTOGRAPHY

Main picture:
River Inagh, Co. Galway, Ireland
ACE/Edmund Nagele

Front cover:
King's College Chapel, Cambridge. John Knox's House, Edinburgh

Back cover:
Caernarfon Castle, Wales. Peterborough Cathedral. Walsingham, Norfolk
DAVID MARSHALL

ISBN 1 873796 12 9
First published in 1993

AUTUMN HOUSE
Alma Park, Grantham, Lincs., NG31 9SL, England

Pilgrim Ways

CONTENTS

Creevykeel	Prehistoric sites
Durrow	Sites associated with Columba
Slane	Sites associated with Patrick
Cashel	Other Celtic sites
ROSSLARE	Places of Interest

Dedication
to Anita

PILGRIMAGE INTO THE PAST

SUN-BLEACHED BEACHES backed by ten-storey, tombstone-like hotels may be some people's idea of a holiday. For three weeks the pressures are off. The most energetic thing they want to do is to apply some Factor Five to the portion of the anatomy next to be exposed to the bronzing rays (and worry about the ozone layer later).

Others look for more. At home or abroad they go in search of history and heritage. Here in the British Isles, the package tour companies are all too pleased to be of service. They arrange a packed programme of castles, cathedrals and stately homes, and herd and harass the bedazed and bewildered until, in a state of utter confusion, they convince themselves that they have 'done' Ireland, or Britain, or Scotland, or wherever.

For the thinking holiday maker in search of history or heritage or something to stimulate the imagination, the package tour method will never suffice. He needs space and leisure and locations away from the beaten tourist track. If he's a Christian or, at least, conscious that Ireland and Britain nursed Christianity not far removed from its cradle, he will want to visit the places where it was nurtured. To see the Ireland of St. Patrick, recall an age when Armagh was the ecclesiastical centre of the British Isles, and Canterbury's cathedral belonged to the mists of the future.

He may want to follow Columba as he crossed the narrow seas in his coracle, and track his missionaries setting out from Iona to take the Gospel to Scotland's glens and lowlands — and then to England and to Gaul.

On the way south he may spend a few days in Aidan's Lindisfarne and Caedmon's Whitby. If he's energetic he may take on the Pembrokeshire coast path to St. David's.

Any pilgrimage to sites of religious significance in Britain would have to take in Canterbury — perhaps across the Pilgrim Way that traverses the North Downs from Alfred the Great's capital, Winchester. No one can savour the great age of ecclesiastical building without visiting Lincoln, Durham, York, Salisbury, Norwich, Westminster Abbey, St. Paul's — and a great many more — and then Rievaulx, Fountains and Jervaulx, ruined abbeys deep in the Dales.

The Reformation trail will take the modern pilgrim to the Edinburgh of John Knox, to Cambridge where Erasmian ideas became the doctrines of reformers, to Tyndale's Gloucestershire and to Oxford where reformers were burned — and Methodism was born.

The Wesley trail alone could take many months. Epworth would have to precede Oxford; then scores of locations in London, Bristol, Cornwall and Yorkshire.

There are the places touched by the lives of great Christians of more recent times. John Bunyan's Bedfordshire. John Newton's Olney. The London of George Whitefield, Charles Spurgeon, and Martyn Lloyd Jones. The trek to Bala in the Welsh mountains tramped by Mary Jones in search of a Bible. David Watson's St. Michael-le-Belfrey, York, home of a modern revival. All Souls next to the BBC, where John Stott lit the fire of contemporary evangelicalism, and where it burns yet. . . .

'It would take more than one lifetime to cover all that ground,' does someone say? No. But it could occupy a good many summer holidays, not to mention weekend breaks and days out. And *any* holiday — or even day out — is the more enjoyable for having an aim. That way it becomes a quest, an adventure.

This is the story of a Christian pilgrimage. Should you wish to follow a part of it, there are certain basic requirements:

A car or, failing that, an up-to-date railway timetable.

Perhaps a guide to bed and breakfast establishments in the area you are going to tackle.

The relevant OS map if you decide to take on one of the hikes or to drive into the remoter regions.

Stout, comfortable footwear, headgear and waterproofs. A backpack is helpful to the long-distance hiker.

A small Bible in your backpack or a slim New Testament about your person. Through the Word, God will speak to you as He has spoken to others in the same locations. Use it in the morning as you set out, and in the evening when you reach base — and in the 101 places you will feel moved to on the way.

Psalm 84 verses 5 and 6 (NEB) will serve to start you off:

> Happy the men whose refuge is in thee,
>> whose hearts are set on the pilgrim ways!
>
> As they pass through the thirsty valley
>> they find water from a spring;
>> and the Lord provides even men who lose their way
>> with pools to quench their thirst.

To be a Pilgrim

In retrospect we might have done it differently. But where is retrospect when you need it?

It all began when I bumped into Buffy Trumpton somewhere in the West One postal district, a patch of old England from whence he rarely strayed. The chance encounter occurred on one of those long, dark days that follow Christmas, and Buffy's spirits were below par.

'Not seen you in yonks,' piped Buffy. 'Why don't we mangle a spot of lunch at Cranks?'

This Trumpton and I went back a long way. When striplings we'd done a stretch together at a certain well-known school and, following our emancipation, had even shared the same institution of higher learning.

At university we had both taken degrees in History, though Buffy had always shown a strong preference for the part that transpired *before* 1066 and myself the part between 1066 and late last night.

Over an ample lunch — his treat — Buffy, in the course of a jog down Memory Lane, reminded me that we had first met at morning prayers in the college chapel. But, as with our historical preferences, religion was another area in which our convictions diverged. Buffy was a High Church man, the son of a bishop, and I a convinced Evangelical.

Half way through dessert Buffy asked me what my plans were for the New Year. I told him that my publishers had invited me to make a year-long pilgrimage around the important religious sites of Britain and Ireland. The idea bucked his spirits instanter. At no timee did he ask if he could accompany me but, long before the bill was paid, it was clear that this man of independent means was about to do just that.

Despite a certain rotundity of form he had acquired around the age of 40, Buffy was not deterred by my announcement that the first leg of my pilgrimage was to be the ancient Pilgrim Way from Winchester to Canterbury.

CHAPTER ONE

STARTING OUT

NOT TEN MILES down the road towards Winchester and we were already thinking we must be mad.

It was a cold, damp, January marrow-bone chiller. Freezing fog had slowed down traffic to walking pace.

Why set out on the 120-mile hike so near the dawn of the year?

'It's the *right* time. Becket was murdered on 29 December 1170,' insisted Buffy, still all enthusiasm. 'And although for 300 years pilgrims tramped the eight to ten-day journey all year round, most liked to tackle it as early in the year as possible. Easter was a favourite time.'

Sensing a let-out clause I was about to start an abandon-mission-until-Easter argument, followed by a burst on my theology — *we* were in search of 'atmosphere', medieval pilgrims were after spiritual credits — when Buffy turned on the car radio.

What we heard made us examine our sanity even more carefully. It was not the weather forecast promising snow we half expected. It was the familiar voice of a newscaster with an unfamiliar — almost unseemly — headlong ebullience in his tone and pace. Twenty-four hours previously the United Nations' deadline for Saddam Hussein to withdraw from Kuwait had expired. The RAF, together with the air forces of 'our coalition partners', had spent the night precision-bombing airfields, chemical and biological warfare facilities, and other 'targets of strategic importance' all over Iraq.

Apocalypse threatened and *we* were planning to retrace the steps of pilgrims from the age of Geoffrey Chaucer.

As the news reporting became increasingly triumph-alistic and repetitious, Buffy switched off the radio and announced, 'That has to be the most frightful thing I've heard in all my puff.'

From here on in the whole expedition was pure escapism.

Winchester

When the Peugeot fetched up at journey's end the freezing fog was long gone.

Hours before we reached the M3 — which passes within five miles of Winchester — the landscape had lifted its misty veil and allowed a glimpse of her true wonder.

What passes for a ring road around Winchester was thronged with traffic. We wound the Peugeot up the tight corkscrew to the top of a multi-storey car park. Then descended on foot into a compact city criss-crossed with pedestrian precincts following the grid of ancient Roman streets.

Even on a wintry afternoon the charm of this ancient capital city was inescapable. Buildings of varying styles — representing the second half of Winchester's over-2,000-year history — caught the eye at every turn and stimulated the imagination. Here and there was an outcrop of Roman Venta Belgarum.

But for many years before Julius Caesar came, saw, conquered, but decided not to stay, there was a town where Winchester now stands. The reason for the settle-ment? Embosomed in the Hampshire Downs, here was an important crossing point of the River Itchen. As Canterbury represented a focus of traffic from the Kent ports — Dover, Deal, Rye, Richborough, Winchelsea — Winchester served the Isle of Wight and Southampton Water ports. Indeed, the submerged valley of South-ampton Water continued inland to the Valley of Itchen

14

and Winchester. Part of Winchester's importance may also have been its proximity to a certain prehistoric east-west road that linked Salisbury Plain with Dover.

The Winchester to Canterbury section of this prehistoric road was to assume a new significance when the shrine of Thomas à Becket became a magnet for pilgrimage. Hence Pilgrim Way.

The Round Table

When Claudius Caesar and his military commanders — Aulus Plautius and Vespasian — came, saw, conquered and decided to settle in AD43 they were not long in selecting Winchester as an administrative centre. By the following year they were building great walls to enclose 138 acres of land. In the years thereafter they built a typical, durable Roman town.

With the departure of the Romans, Winchester increased in importance *vis-à-vis* other cities. It is possible that the legendary Arthur reigned here in the dark age between the Romans and the coming of the Saxons (but tell it not in Tintagel, nor in the streets of Glastonbury . . .). Certain it is that when Henry VIII entertained the Emperor Charles V in 1522 he took him to Winchester Castle — built by William the Conqueror — to inspect the Round Table. Equally certain it is that the table dates only from the reign of Henry III who was born in the castle, and that the great Tudor had it repainted for Charles's benefit, had the Tudor rose and 'King Arthur' painted in the centre — together with the names of twenty-four knights around the edge. Today it makes an impressive backdrop in the Great Hall.

Winchester's years as a capital city began *circa* 519 when it became capital of Saxon Wessex. After the Norman conquest William made Winchester England's capital and the city embarked upon a golden age of prosperity. As late as 1200 it was looked upon as England's capital city.

A statue of King Alfred the Great (849-99) dominates the long precinct that runs through the centre of

Winchester. In laying claim to Alfred, Winchester is, of course, on solid historical ground. While doubt may be cast on whether a King Arthur from Winchester helped defend Britain against the incursions of the Saxons, there is no doubt whatever that Winchester's King Alfred the Great drove the Danes from Wessex, confining them to eastern England. Equally beyond question is the fact that this enlightened ruler made Winchester a centre for scholarship, founded many monasteries, and was among the first to attempt a translation of sections of the Bible into the Anglo-Saxon vernacular.

High cross and cathedral

We had arrived in early afternoon. A famished sun was nibbling at the overcast. We took our famished selves off in search of an eating place. Jewry Street has a number of high class French and Greek restaurants. We entered one and, from our window seat, watched throngs of gesticulating students pass by, some from Winchester's famous public school, others from the Pilgrim's School, still others from King Alfred's College.

As we set out on the central precinct we realized that we had not sighted the cathedral. But glancing right through an archway near the ancient High Cross, we caught a glimpse of it. By contrast with most cathedrals, this one was built in a hollow. Hence its massive size was all the more surprising when we passed through the archway on to the green. The nave is the longest in Europe except for St. Peter's, Rome. Its squat, single tower bespeaks its Saxon origins, though the present building was erected between 1079 and 1093.

The rail placed around the altar by order of Archbishop Laud in the 1630s is still there. Behind it was a single large candlestick with a message attached to it: 'Pray for peace in the Gulf.'

Buffy harbours the not unreasonable belief that it is impolite to enter God's house without speaking to Him. We knelt before the rail and addressed our petitions to the God of peace who suffers when we suffer, hurts when we hurt, and whose great heart must have been breaking as, once more, the latest death-tech was being employed to devastating effect by a considerable array of nations.

After my 'amen' I became aware of the sound of chanting. In that place of echoes it was difficult to ascertain from whence it came. Then I realized that it emanated from a very ordinary anorak-clad man not three yards away. For a few moments it was as if this were the only sound in that cavernous nave. Then it was drowned by louder, jarring sounds.

Beyond the altar a vast structure of scaffolding reached from cold stone floor to distant arched ceiling. There were planks of wood bestrewn amongst it at all kinds of irregular and dangerous angles. Tea break had ended and men were shouting, chiselling, hammering, much as the original builders and masons must have done 900 years before. Restoration work on an impressive scale was being done on the exterior and interior of this ancient place of worship.

The cathedral has an early association with St. Swithun, tutor to Alfred the Great, and Bishop between 852 and 862 in the days of the Old Minster. Winchester's present-day Dean was eager to tell us Swithun's story. By his own request the saint was buried outside the west door of his minster 'where the rains of heaven might fall upon him'. On 15 July 1093 — now St. Swithun's Day — the relics of the saint had been transferred from the old to the new building. A wet summer would appear to have ensued. According to the Dean, it was believed at the time that heaven registered its disapproval at the moving of the saint's body from its original resting place by showering England with continuous rain for forty days. Hence, we were told, the origin of the St. Swithun's Day legend.

From the stained glass windows we realized that what little light there had been that day was failing. Before dark we aimed to discover the commencement of the Pilgrim Way on the edge of the city. As we exited the west door we looked up at the clouds which packed in great, alarming haste across the dark sky. Perhaps some of St. Swithun's rain was about to be transferred from July to January. Using C. J. Wright's *A Guide to The Pilgrim's Way* (Constable), we threaded our way from street to street, landmark to landmark, until we reached a small parish church on Nun's Road. By the side of this church was a stream and on its right bank the path that is the inauspicious beginning of the Pilgrim Way to distant Canterbury.

A freezing drizzle began to fall. We made our way back to the car through the seethe of rush-hour Winchester. It was with difficulty that we guided our car to the overnight billet. The BBC were reporting Iraqi Scud missile attacks on Tel Aviv and Haifa in neutral Israel.

In our dreams the endless rumble of heavy traffic on the road outside became impacting Scuds, Patriots and Cruise Missiles, and the distant thunder of Armageddon.

CHAPTER TWO

The Pilgrim Way

UNUSUALLY, BUFFY WAS up and out betimes to examine the prospects for the day. As I descended to breakfast he came leaping towards me dripping with momentous news.

In the night, rain had clawed the windows, and wind slapped the walls. But now the sun was beaming its greetings from a cloudless sky. Given the time of year it was ideal weather for hiking. Buffy accepted it as an answer to his prayers. In its enthusiasm to report the escalating Gulf War, the BBC had failed completely to forecast the arrival of an anticyclone over the south of England.

At 9am we passed the car — still covered with a thick crust of ice — and, suitably shod, hatted and attired — set off on the Pilgrim Way. Buffy was possessed of OS maps and guide book and read aloud as we tramped.

After a mile or two of paved way the trail became a farm track. We were still following the course of the river. There were swans at first, then a large number of assorted ducks and moorhens. None were swimming, upturning or disporting themselves in accustomed fashion. They were squatting on the bank facing the sun — perhaps the first of the year — and, from time to time, preening themselves.

Before too long we ran up against the first of a number of obstacles.

Oblivious to a thousand years of history, a smallholder had erected a five-barred gate across the Pilgrim Way and had slapped 'Private. Keep Out' upon it. In case we should have been tempted to ignore this warning, there were five snarling dogs threatening to breakfast on us on the other side of the gate. 'It's like something out of John Bunyan,' observed Buffy.

As we came up to the five-barred gate we noticed a rickety bridge across the river. On the other side was a narrow grass track on the left bank.

While crossing the bridge we glimpsed an idyllic, whitewashed, thatched cottage hiding coyly among the trees. We stopped to stare. The earth was steaming after the night's rain, and daffodils were pushing through. Winter aconites made a brilliant yellow carpet beneath the trees.

Jane Austen country

The ambitious leylandii hedge squeezed us to the river's edge and kept us in chilling shade. For a time we listened to the cornflake crunch of frosted grass beneath our feet. Then, suddenly, the track led across open country.

Here the rivers Itchen, Alre and Wey made a sort of watershed. To the winter pilgrim this meant a quagmire, though not, with the sun waxing warmer by the minute, a Slough of Despond. At Alresford the walls of the church — rain-sodden for months, and frosted overnight — steamed visibly. As, indeed, pausing for rest and refreshment, did we.

The twenty-eight-mile section of the Pilgrim Way from Winchester to Farnham is, in fact, a spur off the prehistoric Salisbury Plain to Dover Road that went via Canterbury. Hence this section owes its existence entirely to pilgrims. The OS maps mark the Pilgrim Way clearly. However, across the miles of the ill-drained Itchen Valley we could not help but think that the medieval pilgrims must have used a variety of routes to Alton depending upon the state of the terrain.

Near Alton, Buffy, still showing no sign of the various ills of which he would later complain, insisted that our route should detour to take in the unspoilt, old-world village of Chawton. Here Jane Austen lived from 1809 to 1817 and wrote most of her novels. Her redbrick corner house is now the centrepiece of the village.

Though late afternoon, the sun was still almost hot but, because of its angle, sharp on the eyes.

After Alton it was behind us, throwing our lengthening shadows forward until they made us look like giants. Here we were joined by other hikers making for billets in Farnham. For the first time the uphill stretch of bridle-path that sliced a broad way through the hilltop woodland lived up to our expectations of the Pilgrim Way.

The wolves of exhaustion were upon us as we staggered up Castle Street, Farnham. In the dining-room of the hostel the TV was still recycling the same war news.

Returning from a chat with the landlady, Buffy announced: 'April, May and June are the best months for the Pilgrim Way. The hotels and hostels are less full than in high summer.'

Now, in mid-January, we appeared to have the place to ourselves.

To Guildford

If a Scud missile had hit Farnham overnight I should have slept through it. What *did* awaken me was the noise of Farnham market beneath the window. The high pressure was holding and, once again, we were to be blessed with near perfect conditions for hiking.

Wide Castle Street, off the main A31, was thronged with market stalls, and bustle and old-world charm. The climbing street, lined on the right by ancient almshouses, was dominated by the castle. We struggled up to see it. While the castle itself was 'Open Only On Wednesdays', we were able to explore both the outer and inner courtyards. The former afforded breathtaking views of the town to the south, and the North Downs to the west and east.

Before taking to the open road we visited St. Andrew's church, sitting a while in the many-coloured light of the sun beaming through a beautiful stained glass window. After a time of prayer Buffy began, for the first time, to complain of blisters and to lose some of his vim. I allowed him ten minutes to bathe his feet in white spirit.

The North Downs sprawl the full distance from Salisbury Plain to the Channel coast, almost scraping the edge of the metropolis as they pass by Croydon.

After Farnham we felt we really *were* on the Pilgrim Way, and Buffy forgot to grouse for a mile or two. The track follows the chalk escarpment as far as Charing, only six miles from Canterbury. For most of the eleven miles from Farnham across Hog's Back to Guildford the track follows the top of the escarpment. Beyond Guildford the trackway follows the south side of the scarp, away from the wind and the weather.

Looking north from the top of the scarp as it approaches Guildford — Buffy dragging his feet as if in irons — we could see for miles. Now clouds were beginning to cast huge shadows over the plain below. When we first caught sight of Guildford just one building stood out bathed in sunshine: the modern cathedral. It was the sight of this that caused Buffy to forget his afflictions and suggest a detour. Before we took the winding road down the chalk scarp towards the city we took one last glance at the gentle undulations and forest to the south.

Guildford is a fascinating and ancient town with a steep cobbled high street, an old castle and a quaint sixteenth-century guildhall with a magnificent overhanging clock. But it was to the modern cathedral — consecrated 1961 — that we made our way.

The cathedral is built on a vast green table-land overlooking the city. Spaciously impressive it is an indication of how modern man, like his medieval predecessor, can put the best of his skills into erecting a structure to the greater glory of God.

The impression is one of clean lines and space. There is a high vaulted ceiling in the huge nave with an impressive altar and behind it a single stained glass window. The organ played throughout the hour or so we spent in contemplation there. I felt that it would be possible for even the most convinced anti-modernist — Buffy was a case in point — to lose his prejudices in this great house of God.

But it was well into the afternoon, and time was pressing. In company with a small crowd of evening strollers we rejoined the Pilgrim Way in the village of Shere. Here the Way drops down a steep hill, crosses the churchyard and a bridge, and passes through a copse into the crouched buildings of the ancient village.

Clustered around the church was a film crew. A single artist was painting the pilgrims as they clumped down from the escarpment.

It was from a hill above the village that we saw the sunset. At first there were horizontal blades of vermilion as the dying sun caught the clouds. Then the red deepened against a background of subtle shades of green. Finally, just before the sun dropped below the rim of the horizon, the entire western sky was a rich plum-purple.

In the darkness we hurried on to our billet in Dorking. After dinner we climbed Box Hill. The weather had changed. The rain slanted by in a fine, steely, mysterious haste, emerging out of the gulf of darkness.

The following morning we returned to the promontory known as Newland's Corner and, through the mist, caught a breathtaking view of a deep, long, totally grass-clad valley with one solitary farm and a single track — the Pilgrim Way — in the valley bottom. Within minutes the silent, rippling veils of rain had obscured the view completely.

We considered our options. To give him his due, Buffy, ancient Brit to the core, left the decision to me. He also spared a thought for the ancient pilgrims whose only option would have been to continue tramping the chalky hills towards Canterbury. Perhaps for the first time we caught an inkling of the powerful force that drove them on.

CHAPTER THREE

THE ROAD TO CANTERBURY

THE MEDIEVAL PILGRIM was, in theory at least, a penitent. He wore garments that marked him out as such, and was not allowed to wear shoes or carry a weapon however difficult or dangerous the road. He was not to carry money for even the bare necessities of the journey, but to beg food and shelter along the way.

This devout model is not, of course, the one we find in Geoffrey Chaucer's *Canterbury Tales*. The tales themselves were ribald stories told by the 'pilgrims' to while away the long hours. Nevertheless there are many clues in Chaucer that he was describing *real* people on *real* pilgrimages.

The pilgrims whose progress Chaucer (1343-1400) was relating, however, did not follow the ancient Winchester to Canterbury route. They started out at 'The Tabard', Southwark, and followed Watling Street to Canterbury by way of Rochester.

Chaucer himself had, almost certainly, taken this five-day journey in 1386 to pray for the recovery of his wife Philippa from a serious illness. Had he taken his journey of faith from Winchester to Canterbury, the 120 miles would have taken him between eight and eleven days. If the weather had not decisively interrupted *our* pilgrimage, the distance might well have taken us longer than that. Even with the aid of OS maps finding the route was, in some stretches, far from easy. And then there was the rerouting necessitated by the building of the M20 and M25 in the last forty miles of the journey. The

Pilgrim Way was certainly more easily traversable on foot in Chaucer's century.

Thomas à Becket's Shrine

Chaucer was, at various times, gentleman's attendant to Edward III, Controller of Customs at the Port of London and MP for Kent. He lived at the height of Canterbury's popularity as a place of pilgrimage. For 300 years following Becket's murder in 1170, Canterbury was regarded as among the four great places of pilgrimage in Europe. Two feast days, as well as Easter, would have drawn pilgrimages to Becket's shrine: 29 December, the date of his murder; and 7 July, the date on which (in 1220) Becket's body had been moved to a shrine behind the high altar in Canterbury Cathedral.

Becket was raised to prominence as a result of his friendship with Henry II. For years the King had been in conflict with the Church. The appointment of his worldly, complacent friend Becket as Archbishop of Canterbury was intended by Henry to seal the State's dominance of the Church. But the King had miscalculated. On the instant of Becket's consecration he ceased to be the King's man and became God's man. The King's conflict with the Church continued. Now he had a more formidable foe.

On a night late in December 1170 Henry II of England, at a castle near Bayeux, was in one of his royal rages. Not unusually he was raging about Becket. To the knights who surrounded him, and anyone else who was listening, he shouted: 'What sluggard wretches, what cowards have I brought up in my Court, who care nothing for their allegiance to their master! Not one will deliver me from this low-born priest!'

However Henry had intended his words to be taken, four of his knights took them as a challenge. They crossed the channel to England. A day later Becket sat down to dinner in the hall of the Archbishop's palace, which was separated from the cathedral by the Great Cloister.

Not long after dinner was concluded the clattering of horses was heard in the courtyard outside. Four knights rode into the hall. Moments earlier Becket had entered an adjoining room and was now seated on a couch in conversation with a large group of monks. He was 52, over six feet in height, and spare of physique. The knights burst in upon him. There were raised voices. Crowds of monks and servants pressed around the person of Becket. The knights roared at them but they refused to move. In the ensuing pandemonium the knights ran out of the door shouting, 'To arms, to arms!'

It was 5pm and the winter darkness had fallen. The knights put on their armour. The monks bolted the doors. Becket sat down again on his couch. Knowing what the knights were about, the monks ran along the cloister for sanctuary in the cathedral. Some forced Becket against his will to do the same. Half pushed, half lifted, he was taken through the cloisters and into the dark church where vespers had just begun.

There was a loud hammering at the cathedral door that echoed throughout the nave. By now only three men remained with the Archbishop. They tried to persuade him to hide in the crypt. He refused. Instead he mounted the steps in the north transept. The knights, covered in chain mail, broke into the cathedral.

'For the name of Jesus, and the defence of the Church, I am ready to die,' whispered Becket. With these words he fell flat on his face. At this, one of the knights delivered a tremendous blow that severed the top of his skull. The blow was so violent that the sword snapped as it met the floor. Within minutes a violent thunderstorm broke over Canterbury.

While the thunder was in progress a strange scene was taking place before the high altar of the cathedral. The monks were undressing the body of Becket for burial. They found that it was covered by an incredible assortment of garments. Apparently the Archbishop had suffered from the cold. Eventually they came to the robe of a Benedictine monk. Then, to their greater surprise, when they had completely stripped the body, they discovered that Becket had worn a hair shirt next to his skin and that beneath it his body was marked with the weals of scourging.

Soon word spread throughout the ecclesiastical community, then out into the city — and beyond to London. The Archbishop had been the most austere monk in England! Within hours of his martyrdom, Thomas à Becket was hailed as St. Thomas of Canterbury.

A number of monks had witnessed his martyrdom. They, with others, wrote detailed accounts of it. These accounts spread largely by word of mouth through Europe.

The curious mixture of emotions that made up Henry II caused him to submit, naked, to the scourging of the monks of Canterbury as he knelt before the high altar. This, too, added drama to the Becket story.

Miracles were attributed to St. Thomas à Becket. Soon thousands annually were tramping in pilgrimage to his shrine. Most trudged the Pilgrim Way from Winchester. But, at the height of the age of pilgrimage and the cult of Becket, during the age of Chaucer, they trudged from all directions, including 'The Tabard', Southwark.

'The Darling Buds of May'

We had abandoned our January pilgrimage at Dorking. During the night following our return, silent snows possessed the earth. A fortnight's freeze followed. Buffy Trumpton opined that not even the hardiest pilgrim would have carried on to Canterbury under these conditions . . . .

It was early May when commitments took me to ancient Rye. Built on a high, sea-facing hill, the 'port' of Rye is now three miles inland. Its narrow, cobbled, steep streets are lined with the homes of writers and artists. A plaque outside one house indicated that it had been the home of novelist H. E. Bates. Recalling his *Darling Buds of May*, a story of Kentish country life against a backdrop of apple and cherry blossom time, the hiking urge came upon me. Phoning the West One postal district I suggested to Buffy that we complete the pilgrimage to Canterbury. His blisters forgotten, he said, 'Let's smack into it *tout de suite!*'

The North Downs past Dorking were swathed in a richer green now and, minus January's mud and chill winds, hiking was pure pleasure. On the wide-open downland between Dorking and Merstham sheep nibbled grass, and beech-hangers edged the valleys. There was the smell of chalk, and pink blossom trees lined the streets of every village.

Grand houses and estates occasionally interrupted the straight course of the downland path. Among them was the great mansion of Chevening. It was here that Buffy caught up with me.

At Otford, just north of Seven Oaks, we came across the first of a number of ruined archbishops' palaces. The medieval church boasted a chain of palaces from London to Canterbury. In an age when roads were dangerous such 'palaces' were partly safe-houses, each containing a small army of retainers, grooms and baggage porters to accompany the archbishop and his guests as they made their way between Canterbury and London. The ruins of four such palaces — Otford, Wrotham, Maidstone and Charing — stand directly on the Pilgrim Way. All went into decline at the Reformation. But the Otford palace was to see its finest hour under the archbishopric of Thomas Cranmer. Cranmer provided lavish entertainment for Henry VIII and Queen Katherine, with a retinue of 5,000, when they were *en route* to France. Today only ruins remain; the tower is open to the sky, and birds nest in every cavity.

Each of our mornings began early; the sun rising, the birds singing and the grass steaming. The two miles between Otford and Kemsing represent, without question, an authentic stretch of the original Way. Beyond Kemsing the Pilgrim Way became a pleasant country lane. At St. Clere we encountered another Stuart mansion within sight of the Way. At Wrotham we were disappointed that the archbishop's palace had been so completely demolished. Among hills largely covered by the rich yellow of oilseed rape, Wrotham was essentially old world. Oast houses dotted the fields.

We were now in H. E. Bates country. The map showed that motorways were not far away, but for miles we caught neither sight nor sound of them. The Way went between fields of green and yellow or along paved paths overhung completely by green trees.

In our January journey 'Pilgrim Way' signs were in short supply. Not so now. At Trottiscliffe there was even a Pilgrim House.

Not far from Maidstone we found the most delightful surprise of all. The Way passed by the grand estate surrounding Leeds Castle, an excuse for a detour.

Leeds Castle is one of England's most romantic buildings. It contains royal apartments of the medieval period; and royals of a variety of nationalities and over many centuries have lodged here or met here to consult.

What sets Leeds Castle apart from the rest is that it is built in the middle of a large lake and joined to the shore by an arched bridge. The imposing gate tower is Norman.

And so to Canterbury

The last lap of the Pilgrim Way — the sixteen miles from Charing to Canterbury — is a well-beaten path. At times I wondered if Buffy was going to make it. Periodically a throaty growl as of a Rocky Mountain timber wolf would be emitted. His blisters were playing him up.

Out of Charing we had plenty of company. This was Kent in apple-blossom time. And there was field after gently undulating, south-facing field of small evenly-spaced, well-pruned apple trees — all in full blossom. Every now and then along the way there was a bank of cherry blossom, the luxurious pink dazzling the eye. Very occasionally there was the yellow of laburnum.

Pilgrim Way passes through the picturesque village of

Chilham with its timbered houses and fifteenth-century church.

As we took the Way south of the church, distant hills dotted with oast houses, we could almost catch the scent and sound and exhilaration of the ancient pilgrims as they trod the last few miles into Canterbury.

Bulldozing the present from our minds we tried to see the great cathedral as thousands of pilgrims, centuries ago, must have seen it.

Today the Seat of St. Augustine is clustered around with other large buildings that detract from its splendour. In medieval times much of what is now Canterbury would have been a wooden shanty town affording an unobstructed view. The streets immediately around the cathedral, like Mercery Lane, are medieval in origin. And, having entered the ancient northern gate of the city as we did, the pilgrims would have trudged these narrow streets, the upper storeys overhanging, and happening upon the Cathedral green must have thought the great edifice the grandest in the world. Few of them would have seen one grander.

The Cathedral Church of Christ at Canterbury is still the focal point for the religious aspirations of millions of Christians in many parts of the world.

The modern pilgrim enters the cathedral precincts by the Christ Church Gate, the earliest example of a late Gothic building incorporating Renaissance touches. Entering the cathedral by the south-west porch the first view that greets him of the grand interior is the magnificent Perpendicular Nave, completed some 230 years after Becket's murder. But, to the left of the nave, down half a dozen steps, more centuries are swept away. There is the very door upon which the merciless knights made their entrance in the dark evening of 1170. There is the spot where Becket fell. The point of his martyrdom is now commemorated by the Altar of the Sword's Point, dominated by the Sword's Point sculpture.

Beyond, and down more steps, more centuries slip away. There is the crypt. On a spot near here, centuries before Thomas à Becket was born, the first Latin primate, St. Augustine, baptized King Ethelbert of Kent. This baptism, on Whit Sunday 597, symbolized the first official acceptance of Roman Christianity in what would become known as England.

The crypt is still a place of prayer. Beneath its altar Becket lies buried. Before its altar medieval pilgrims by the thousand did their penance — and Henry II received his whipping.

Above, in the nave and in the side-chapels near the tombs of the Black Prince and King Henry IV, curiously adjacent, devout Christians pray. Not, now, for peace. The Gulf War has receded into history and, like all wars, has left horrendous problems in its wake. The nation of the Kurds is on the move in the mountains, escaping one tyrant to suffer starvation and die from exposure. In Ethiopia and the Horn of Africa seventeen million are threatened with death from famine. In Bangladesh hundreds of thousands are dead and homeless after a cyclone.

The politics of Becket pale and — irony of ironies — the immense cost of maintaining the ecclesiastical pile that covers the place of his burial, competes for the contents of the pockets of modern 'compassion-fatigued' pilgrims. . . .

CHAPTER FOUR

CORNWALL IN BLOOM

BUFFY, THAT SON of a bishop, was not so keen on Cornwall when first I suggested a visit. He suspected me of wanting to follow the Wesley trail. When I hinted that we should take along our wives and make a holiday of it, he was raring to go.

As things turned out we could not have picked a better time to visit Cornwall. It was the last week in May and the county was in bloom. And Mrs. Buffy — bless her heart! — was a wild-flower enthusiast, as, indeed, was Anita. Our wives were in for the time of their lives. Buffy, as always, enjoyed himself in a moderate sort of way. With the exception, that is, of a day on which we nearly finished him off. More of that anon.

Wesley's Cornwall

TREWINT. No sooner were we past Launceston than we were into countryside stuffed full of flowers. The grassy banks of the narrow lanes could not have been more colourful. In some areas bluebells predominated. Elsewhere it was red campion, white campion and cow parsley. Tree-proportioned hedges of fresh white may filled the air with delicate scent. As the lanes opened up into gentle moorland, vivid yellow gorse provided the backdrop for acres of buttercups intermingled with campion.

Buffy had nodded off when, with the connivance of the wives, I detoured off the A30 into the ancient village of Trewint. He was hardly awake when we ushered him through a door into the coolth of a one up, one down cottage wedged awkwardly between two full-size cottages. He rumbled our conspiracy when, having taken a seat, the cheeriest and politest of Cornish voices asked him please not to sit on that chair, it was Wesley's.

Mrs. Buffy was hugely amused by the alacrity with which he shot up and, wide-eyed, examined the ancient chair on which he had been sitting. A Methodist herself, she beamed as her beloved peered with something that bordered on reverence at the Wesley prints that lined the passage, the open fireplace where John and Charles kept warm when wild winds blew unhindered across Bodmin Moor, and at the bed and Wesleyan memorabilia upstairs.

No one believed me (at first, anyway) that I was as surprised as anyone at what greeted us when, after a half-hour's thoughtful examination of the tiny cottage, we emerged back into the blistering heat of the day. *We were facing a legion of Methodists.* Against the longest odds we had arrived on Wesley Day (24 May).

Fifteen minutes later, scrunched in among the Methodist front row, heads bare to the merciless grill of the sun, we were listening to an amply-proportioned, period-dressed preacher (who spoke from the shade of a porch).

Wesley Day was, we learned, the anniversary of that summer day in 1743 when two of Wesley's travelling preachers had stopped at the tiny hamlet of Trewint on the edge of Bodmin Moor. They had asked for refreshment at 'yonder house, where the stone porch is'. Digory and Elizabeth Isbell, who dwelt within, had been more than pleased to entertain the two strangers for the night. Next morning Digory had been 'mazed' when, leaving a shilling, the preachers knelt and prayed for the home and the Isbell family — 'without a book'!

John Wesley heard of the hospitality of Digory and Elizabeth and began to board in their home himself. As Cornwall gradually became 'Wesley's County', Digory, a stonemason, built two additional rooms between his own and the neighbouring cottage, a 'Prophets' Chamber' where John and Charles Wesley and the Methodist preachers could stay over as and when they pleased. It was from Trewint, we learned, that the Wesleyan revival was launched in Cornwall. Methodist societies had originally been established among the tinners around Gwennap, Redruth, Pool, Camborne, Hayle, St. Ives and St. Just. It had been tin and copper mining that had made possible the building of the large chapels in those districts. However, eventually, as the revival had spread throughout the county, chapels of various shapes and sizes had been built in virtually every town, village and hamlet.

We had chosen the right day to visit Trewint. However, we were told that this shrine of Methodism is open to the public almost every day of the year.

GWENNAP PIT. Buffy Trumpton's relations were both numerous and ubiquitous. During our round-Britain-pilgrimage this was to prove a plus. It was, perhaps, inevitable that there should have been Trumptons in Cornwall. Hence we were able to use their extensive bungalow at Port Isaac as our base. In Port Isaac we picked up a copy of Thomas Shaw's *A Methodist Guide to Cornwall*, containing a map showing the locations of the hundreds of Methodist chapels and, in alphabetical order, telling the story of the revival in each locality.

At nearby Port Gaverne, grass banks sheened blue with forget-me-nots steeping down to pebbled rivers, we met the Methodist superintendent. Like the Trewint speaker, he wore a ground-length black gown, with a cord round his middle and Wesley-type neckwear. Out of Buffy's hearing he told us that anyone on the Wesley trail could not afford to miss the meeting at Gwennap Pit to take place on Bank Holiday Monday (three days hence). We resolved to be there.

Finding it was to prove quite a problem. Buffy was suggesting a score of more interesting places to visit. Hence the ladies navigated us there. The nearest town is Redruth. Gwennap is just off the A393 near Carharrack.

Gwennap Pit is a natural amphitheatre caused by

mining subsidence. In Wesley's honour it was landscaped ten years after his death. It now consists of twelve circles of turfed seats decreasing in size from top to bottom. On at least eighteen occasions Wesley addressed thousands here. Since his death in 1791 Methodists from all over the world have gathered to hear his gospel and sing his brother's hymns (and a few of his own). This annual gathering is now held on Spring Bank Holiday.

It was in this international assemblage of Methodists that we found ourselves. Buffy fidgeted at first and expressed a preference for plain chant over Wesley hymns. Nevertheless, during 'Oh for a thousand tongues to sing', he lifted his rich bass voice to his 'great Redeemer's praise'.

ST. IVES AND ST. AGNES. St. Ives and St. Agnes were strong Methodist centres during and well beyond Wesley's lifetime.

Riots and stonings had greeted the Wesley brothers when they had first preached in St. Ives. However, by the time John was in his eighties the town was almost 100 per cent Wesleyan. On his way to preach there he encountered an adventure, the story of which continues to be told there and is recounted in his *Journal*. Crossing the Hayle Estuary to address the population of St. Ives one evening he was told that he was in great danger. A stiff wind was blowing in from the sea, the road had disappeared into the sands, water half covering the wheels of the carriage, and it was difficult to see the way ahead. Realizing the danger, postilion Peter Martin stopped the carriage; 'I advised Mr. Wesley of the danger of the crossing,' he wrote. The captain of a vessel awaiting the turn of the tide saw them. And came up 'to dissuade us from an undertaking so full of peril'.

Wesley politely told them that he had to keep his appointment to preach and, from the carriage window, called to Martin, 'Take the sea! Take the sea!' Martin spurred the horses forward. The waters swirled; 'The horses were now swimming, and the carriage became nearly overwhelmed with the tide, as its hinder wheels not infrequently merged into the deep pits and hollows in the sand,' writes Martin. 'I struggled hard to maintain my seat in the saddle, while the poor afrighted animals were snorting and rearing in the most terrific manner, and furiously plunging through the opposing waves. I expected every moment to be swept into eternity, and the only hope of escape I then cherished was on account of my driving so holy a man.' He heard Wesley call to him; 'What is thy name, driver?'

'Peter.'

'Peter, fear not: thou shalt not sink!' shouted Wesley.

Wesley put back his head and Peter urged the horses. They got safely over, 'but it was a miracle', wrote Peter.

At St. Ives, both men were drenched. Wesley arranged a change of clothes and refreshment for Martin but, his own clothes sodden, he proceeded to preach to the receptive multitude.

Wesley regarded St. Agnes as a particular challenge, preaching there nineteen times. The Celtic Church had been founded there in AD450 but, in the eighteenth century, it was one of the industrial centres of Cornwall. A large number of mines could be found in the area.

Celtic Cornwall

The Celtic Christianity that abounded in Britain and Ireland before Augustine is associated with the names of Patrick and Columba. Hence we expect to find evidence of the Celtic Church in Scotland, Ireland, Wales and the extreme north of England. Buffy Trumpton, for one, was surprised to find so much evidence of the Celtic Church in Cornwall.

The saints after whom Cornwall has named its towns and villages were *Celtic* saints.

'Perhaps that was why Wesley went over big round here,' said Buffy.

'Not in the positive way you imply,' said I. 'Though I think there is a connection.'

'Don't follow your drift,' said Buffy.

'Then I'll snow a bit more,' said I.

36

The parish churches in Cornwall are, in the main, built on the sites of Celtic shrines. That is why, in so many instances, they are distant from the villages. Cornishmen contemporary with Wesley claimed that many in the county were married and buried without benefit of clergy. The weakness of Anglicanism in Cornwall helped Methodism to prosper. The remoteness of the diocesan, the Bishop of Exeter, meant that there was inadequate supervision of clergy. Hence too many were lazy, drunken, and cared little for their parishioners. The lack of clerical restraint may also account for the evidence that Cornwall's tin miners and fishermen often turned to smuggling and wrecking.

TRURO. Not until 1876 was a bishopric established — at Truro — in Cornwall. Not until 1910 was the beautiful cathedral at Truro completed. On the Sunday we visited the city its heat-soaked streets were empty. We had the cathedral to ourselves for the afternoon. Among its stained glass, carved wood, and bold, lofty dimensions, Buffy felt spiritually at home.

ST. COLUMB. Over the fireplace in the bungalow that was our temporary home was a large map of Cornwall. In the evenings, after we had all watched the sun go down from the sands at Polzeath, Mrs. Buffy and Anita would study this map and work out our itinerary for the following day.

It was Mrs. Buffy who noticed that not far away from our billet were no less than three villages incorporating the name St. Columb. The largest was St. Columb Major. We arrived at its parish church one Sunday morning at 10am. Bells rang out from the tower and we went in to pray.

The church, like the town, was dedicated to St. Columb. For a parish church it was extremely impressive. It had, as we later discovered, an equally impressive set of records.

The question in our minds was this: Could 'St. Columb' be a slight corruption of St. Columba, the great Celtic saint of Ireland and Scotland?

37

As we delved into the history of the church and town we ran up against a most implausible legend. This late-date romantic story had St. Columb as a woman! A woman who, nevertheless, had been a Celtic missionary from Ireland.

However, as the local historians were the first to admit, it was entirely possible that the story of the great St. Columba had been carried by the Celtic missionaries to Cornwall and that it was *his* name that was commemorated in the three place names in the area.

PADSTOW AND ST. PETROC. First light on another morning found us in St. Petroc's churchyard on the edge of Padstow. Petroc, we discovered, had connections with Lindisfarne. On his long journey from Northumbria to Cornwall he had been among the founders of a religious centre at Sherborne in the Yeo Valley. The present-day abbey at Sherborne was built over the site of an earlier Celtic abbey. Sherborne had been the centre of the Celtic Church in the south-west until the Saxon invasion of 658.

But, having established this connection, this is as far as we got — historically speaking — with Padstow.

Outside the dank church, the sun was warm and the sea was beckoning. Everywhere we looked Cornwall was in full bloom. On the walk from Trevone to Constantine every sea-facing cliff and hill was covered with sea-pinks. On our way back we found the lanes banked with valerian. A whole field was covered with bright yellow ragwort.

Near Constantine, Buffy found a golf course. And, for that day, we had lost him. Returning to Padstow the three of us decided on another trek. This time it was over the cliffs to the wide sands of the Camel Estuary. On the other side, at Rock, was a church dedicated to another Celtic saint, St. Enodoc. This church, half covered with sand, captured the imagination of poet John Betjeman who lived nearby.

TINTAGEL AND BOSCASTLE. Since our arrival in Cornwall both Anita and Buffy's lady had insisted on a visit to Tintagel 'to find King Arthur'.

What we actually found at Tintagel was, to us, considerably more exciting than King Arthur! When the 'rebuilding' of Tintagel Castle had begun in 1852 a Roman milestone had been discovered bearing the name of the Emperor Licinius (AD308-324). Nearby a chapel dedicated to Cornwall's patron saint St. Piran — another Celtic saint — was excavated. Near it was found another Roman milestone, this one naming Gallus and Volusian (251-253). The excavations by Dr. C. A. Ralegh Radford had discovered remains on the island on which 'King Arthur's castle' stands, evidence of a Celtic monastery that had been in use from the fifth to the ninth centuries. Here, in pagan Saxon England, had been an enclave of Christianity probably under the protection of a Cornish king.

Half a mile away, near the present-day parish church, Charles Thomas of the Institute of Cornish Studies has recently been excavating what have always been believed to be Roman earth works. In the course of his excavations he has found that the 'earth works' were in fact Celtic burial mounds from the fifth century. The Celtic stone coffins are now on show.

For beauty it is difficult to beat Boscastle. Novelist Thomas Hardy poked around among the Celtic excavations here.

On the instant of our arrival we fell in love with the place. There is an S-bend in the river that winds out to the sea. It is caused by a great mountain of granite — literally covered with sea-pinks on the day of our visit — that shields Boscastle from north winds. Having walked past the quaint, rickety buildings on the riverside, we found a sheltered spot on the sea-pink covered bank — and promptly forgot all about saints and reformers.

In search of St. Piran

Buffy had come to Cornwall after a solemn undertaking on my part that there would be no, *definitely* no long walks. In view of this it had been necessary for me to be somewhat surreptitious in my study of John

Mason's *Walk the Cornish Coastal Path* (a Bartholomew Map and Guide). But it was in the course of my examination of this book that I learned that, between Holywell and Perranporth, the oratory of Cornwall's patron saint, Piran, had been excavated.

It was only after much gentle persuasion from the ladies, together with my assurance that the walk could not possibly be more than three-and-a-half miles that, with the rest of us, Buffy was induced to leave the car at Holywell and set out on the cliff walk to Perranporth ('Piran's Port').

The first stage of our pilgrimage was around the perimeter fence of an army establishment from which came the crackle of gunfire. To keep us to the path that followed the edge of perilous cliffs — and away from the line of fire — the Ministry of Defence had placed a series of white posts. Over a mile or so of coast path, following these posts enabled us to enjoy incredible views of vast cliffs and offshore islands — all completely covered with sea pinks.

Suddenly, as the three-mile beach of Perran Bay began, there were no more white posts. We strayed down on to the beach, but there were no waymarks there. Under searing sun, nude bathers were splashing around in the shallows.

The walk thus far had taken us longer than anticipated and we had overshot lunchtime. Because of the nature of the terrain Buffy was convinced that we had walked at the very least ten miles. Now the cliffs had ended and behind us were sand-dunes as far as the eye could see. According to the map they stretched three miles inland and were labelled Penhale Sands.

Buffy was growling and Mrs. Buffy was wilting. The sun was blistering and there was, it must be admitted, a genuine danger of sunstroke. Tummies rumbled. It was too far to walk back. We struck off into the sand-dunes.

Sand-dunes are hard to climb. Where the coarse grass that held them together ran out, it was a case of one step up, three steps down. And, when you've been clambering over dunes for three-quarters of an hour, one sand-hill looks pretty much like another. After a time we realized that the sand-dunes had reached the height of the cliffs.

Buffy had become an alarming sight, perspiration springing from his nobly bejowled, lobster-coloured visage.

The ladies trudged, heads down, about 200 yards behind me. Buffy, pouring sweat, lost distance by stopping every few yards to take a swig of his 'medicine' ('It's for the heart, you know').

I clambered to the top of the highest sand-hill of all, more or less ready to hoist the white flag. Under extreme heat and fatigue, not having a clue where I was and having definite fears about Buffy's survival potential, I was tending to get a bit desperate.

I shall never forget what met the eye when I reached the top of that sand mountain. A mile or so away, over sand-dunes, shimmering in the heat, I saw the cross.

No, really. There it was, bold against the sky.

This had been the point of maximum discouragement. Sand in every direction. But with the sight of the cross discouragement fled and the heart was lifted. Within twenty minutes we were all atop that sand mountain. We resolved to make a beeline for the cross.

We kept it in view until we were close to it. Then it was temporarily obscured. The way forward appeared, in any case, to be impossible because of a vast coil of barbed wire.

A young man with an ear-ring appeared from nowhere. He asked the way to the beach. Anita pointed, then asked *him* the way to the cross. He began to give complicated directions which, had we followed them, might have kept us in that sand wilderness until this day.

It was then that I noticed there was a way round the barbed wire and, looking back saw a notice indicating that for the last hour we had been on the MOD's firing range.

Beyond the barbed wire we rounded a hill. One final clamber and we were at the foot of the cross.

In a squat building nearby were housed the excavations of Piran's Oratory. The cross marked the cradle of Cornwall's Christianity.

—o—

A bus took us into Perranporth. Behind the three miles of golden sands was a honeycomb of tall 'caves', in fact the remains of the eighteenth-century tin-mine workings.

Buffy was still giving cause for concern. Only after a two-hour rest in the shade of a 'cave' during which he was plied with at least two litres of 'sparkling spring water' by his lady were Buffy's spirits restored.

Anita and I took a turn round the town and, when we returned to the cave, Buffy's capacious form was silhouetted against an enormous deep red sinking sun.

Ever a man for surprises he jumped up and said with enthusiasm, 'Do you realize, in ten days we shall be in Ireland?'

CHAPTER FIVE

ISLE OF SAINTS AND SCHOLARS

THE CHRISTIANITY CENTRED on Canterbury was Roman and introduced to southern Britain by Augustine and his successors. However, when Pope Gregory I appointed Augustine missionary to Britain his task was not only to convert a 'pagan land'. He was commissioned to challenge the form of Christianity which had already taken root in Britain and differed in marked respects from the Roman sort.

When Augustine put ashore on the Isle of Thanet in 597 the Celtic Church was already strong in England, Scotland and parts of Wales.

But its origins are in Ireland. And its founder Ireland's patron saint, Patrick.

Hence the cradle of Christianity in the British Isles is found in Ireland. And any pilgrimage to find the roots of the faith in these isles should follow an itinerary in that slow-paced land of peace and peerless beauty.

Across the sea to Ireland

The day Buffy and I set off for Fishguard was unworthy of June. Low cloud seemed to cover the whole country and the finest mist kept the windscreen wipers in constant use. We saw little of Wales as we sped through.

The three-and-a-half-hour crossing to Rosslare enabled us to get among our multi-national fellow passengers.

Buffy gave the impression he was quite definitely among the *cognoscenti* and dispensed advice to all.

The substance of the chatter below decks seemed to depend on your passport. While Germans, Swedes and Dutch were looking forward to their Irish experience with unqualified enthusiasm, the English and Americans were bothering a bit about things they had heard on the news, what the accommodation would be like, and whether they had been wise to bring a car with an English registration. . . .

On the point of political geography Buffy reassured the ditherers that they could tour Ireland — north and south — 'for months if not years' without a second thought about the few square miles of 'bandit country'. Those who know Ireland best would agree with him. In our tour of Ireland the only place where we saw men with guns (soldiers) was in Armagh, in a bit of a tremor the two days we were there.

As to the question of accommodation and English registration plates on cars, Buffy held his peace. Our experience was to be that the standard of accommodation in Ireland is second to none. Our billets, farms mainly, were five star and would have been twice the price in England. All are listed in the RAC's *Small Hotels and Guest Houses* available from bookshops and updated each year. Breakfasts and evening meals are such that you do not feel the need to eat for the rest of the day. What was to impress Buffy was the warmth of welcome and the conversation — they call it 'crack'.

But as to English registrations on cars. . . . Before we set off Buffy had said: 'Take your own car. No one's going to waste a bomb or a bullet on us.' However, it's not a question of bombs or bullets. British or Ulster registration plates indicate opulence to, among others, the younger generation in Dublin. Further to which, while Ireland's main roads are excellent, side roads are heavily potholed. If you ever spare a thought for your axles and suspension, you might feel easier in your mind if you were driving a car hired in the Republic.

'The Irish experience'

Sealink had outpaced the clammy climate within half an hour of the Welsh coast. The sun shone brightly on the lowlands around Wexford as we put in at Rosslare. Driving up the long, straight Arklow road I had an impression that remained with me throughout our stay in Ireland. The colours of the Irish countryside are so intense that I seemed to be viewing it all through polarized lenses. Short of a cliché, 'forty shades of green' is actually an understatement.

From the second we drove off the ship we had the feeling that we had entered a very different, lush land in which the pace of life was altogether slower and the past and present lived cheek by jowl. In a single burst of speed I overtook a man-led, baggage-laden mule *and* a brand-new, shining Mercedes.

The evening drive to Coolgreany was glorious. Cars are less plentiful in Ireland and, as in Sweden, the main roads are built with lined-off hard shoulders enabling slower vehicles to pull in, thus permitting faster ones to pass by.

Most villages through which we passed had just one wide street. Many of the dwellings on either side had but a single storey. Large groups of men sat out of doors on hard chairs or stood in doorways. The art of conversation is alive and well in Ireland.

Finding our turning off the Arklow road to Coolgreany proved to be a harassing undertaking. Road signs to major destinations are clear, but signs to minor destinations arrive unheralded, the print too small to read. A clear road map and Buffy's navigation were indispensable. Even then a certain amount of tyre tread was left upon the road and some turnings tackled on two wheels . . . .

As we rumbled into Coolgreany a disproportionate number of buildings seemed to be derelict (a feature of the Irish landscape that speaks eloquently of Ireland's history). Swallows flashed from one ruined roof to another, while chickens pecked at the road surface. 'Angels and ministers of grace defend us!' quoth Buffy, looking up from his map and wondering which of the ruined dwellings represented our night's lodging! However, round the corner was a manor house contained in formal gardens and, inside its front door, our first taste of warm, Irish hospitality.

Our first full day was spent in Dublin. O'Connell Street, Phoenix Park, Dublin Castle, Trinity College with its ancient Book of Kells: we saw them all. But, in common with any great city, though out of temper with the rest of Ireland, its streets were traffic-choked and the approach to driving of its inhabitants distinctly kamikaze.

An evening walk enabled us to catch a scent of the atmosphere. The doorway to every pub and bar seemed to let out the sound of accordion, fiddle, or guitar-accompanied folk singing. At our billet the sitting room 'crack' was to a background of Irish folk songs, occasionally sung in Gaelic. Buffy took a real shine to our brisk university-educated landlady who passed among her guests, chatting to each, keeping everybody happy and helping them feel (her words) 'a part of it'. A part of, that is, the unforgettable, inimitable, 'Irish Experience'.

On the trail of St. Patrick

But, looking back, we felt that our Irish adventure began when we were well clear of Dublin's fair city. Poking around in Rush and Skerries on the rain-rinsed coast north of Dublin, we felt we had found the first scent of St. Patrick. One of the four islands off Skerries is St. Patrick's Island where the saint is believed to have landed on his way from Wicklow to Ulster. The ruins of an early monastery (plundered by the Vikings in 795) remains on the island.

If the place of St. Patrick's birth was known it would doubtless be the greatest place of pilgrimage of all. Some believe that he was born at Dumbarton on the Clyde or somewhere nearer the Solway Firth. His birth is likely to have been circa 390 and his Christianization of Ireland took place between 432 and 461. What the Irish call a 'strong tradition' indicates that he was captured as a slave and transported, first to Ireland, and then to Gaul. It is believed that in Gaul he became a convinced Christian and that, having escaped from his captors, he returned to Ireland — bringing Christianity with him. Patrick's first oratory is believed to have been at Saul near the hill where an enormous statue of the great saint now stands. His principal church is believed to have been at Armagh beneath the site of the Church of Ireland Cathedral. A variety of sites in both Ulster and the south of Ireland are associated by ancient tradition with monasteries either founded by Patrick or by one of his successors.

From Skerries we went to Drogheda and followed the course of the river Boyne along the rich, water-fed, tree-lined, meadow-rich valley called King William's Glen.

We examined the scene where the fate of Ireland and of the Stuart dynasty was decided in battle in 1690.

Between alternating sunbursts and sharp showers we examined Monasterboice a few miles west of Drogheda. Here was one of the very early monastic sites associated with the Celtic Church. These ruins of a substantial monastic settlement founded by St. Buithe who died in 521 feature a number of high crosses. The Celtic crosses are sculpted with easily identifiable stories from the Bible. Here we saw the first of many Round Towers. These towers, a feature of the ecclesiastical landscape of Ireland, were originally built to enable monastics to escape the frequent attacks by marauding Vikings.

To reach the Slane abbey ruins we crossed from County Louth to County Meath and climbed Slane Hill (529 feet). It is believed that on this hill, before the chieftains and the High King based at nearby Tara had been converted to Christianity, St. Patrick, in defiance of a royal decree, kindled his first Paschal Fire and celebrated, with his earliest disciples, the Lord's Supper. It is with one of these disciples, St. Earc (who died *circa*

512), that the monastic ruins at Slane are associated.

Today there is little to be seen at Tara. Nevertheless it was once the seat of the pagan priest-kings of Ireland and affords pleasing, though not spectacular, views over the rich, green, patchworked Midlands of Ireland.

In recent years those interested in the pre-Christian history of Ireland have been more concerned with the excavation of the megalithic tomb at Newgrange.

Near to the site of the Battle of the Boyne, Newgrange and the Heritage Centre attached to it are a must for anyone interested in the earliest artefacts of Irish, indeed Western history.

Newgrange is a great chambered mound of turves and stones about 280 feet in diameter and about 44 feet high, constructed *circa* 3100 BC. Serious archaeologists claim that it was built over 5,000 years ago! In other words, that it is older than Stonehenge and belongs to the era of the Pyramids.

The mound is bounded by a retaining kerb of large, horizontally-laid stones bearing splendidly-carved, prehistoric works of art. The structure is designed in such a way as to allow the sun to illuminate the central tomb just once a year, on 21 December, at the time of the winter solstice.

Buffy informed me peremptorily that I could tackle this one on my own and that I was 'a brick shy of a full load' if I went in there. It was a fascinating experience. The reconstruction of the retaining kerb, said the guide, was based on the position of the layers of white quartz stones found in the earlier stage of the excavation after 1962. At the heart of the burial chamber the lights were turned out and gradually the effect of the once-a-year incursion of the sun was simulated by a carefully-placed electric beam.

While in County Meath anyone in search of the Christian roots of the British Isles will want to visit Kells. St. Columba (occasionally spelt Columcille) was the most distinguished successor of St. Patrick. The present-day St. Columba's church covers the site of what was once

The Church of St. Columb in the village of St. Columb Major. The recurrence of the name Columb in Cornwall may suggest a direct connection between Christianity in this south-westerly county and the greatest of the missionaries of the Celtic Church, Columba of Iona.

Magdalen College, Oxford, where the fellows took a strong stand in defence of Anglicanism in 1687-88. Oxford was also the city of Wyclif, and of Wesley.

Each year, on Spring Bank Holiday, Methodists from all over the world come to worship at Gwennap Pit, near Redruth, to recall Wesley's Aldersgate Street conversion.

The coastal path from Holywell to St. Piran's Oratory, Piran being the first missionary to preach the Gospel in Cornwall. The roots of Cornwall's Christianity are among the Celtic saints after whom the county's towns and villages are named.

Winchester Cathedral where the ancient Pilgrim Way begins.

The Bell Harry Tower, Canterbury Cathedral. The 120-mile Pilgrim Way, much trodden in medieval times, ends at the shrine of Thomas á Becket, murdered in 1170.

York Minster, an ancient cathedral in a city which has preserved so much of its fascinating heritage from Roman through Viking times to the Age of Railways.

The Isle of Iona, accessible by boat from Oban and Mull, used as the centre from which Columba and his successors launched Christianity in Scotland, England and Gaul.

Lindisfarne, the Holy Isle off the Northumbrian coast, has its own intriguing story.

Whitby, where a synod decided Christianity's direction in Britain, and Caedmon caught the vision of bringing the Gospel to the people.

The vast monolith of St. Patrick, on a high hill near Saul, Co. Down. A few miles away is the cathedral at Downpatrick where the saint is believed to be buried.

Glendalough, a cradle of Christianity in a lush valley in the Wicklow Mountains.

St. Kevins in Glendalough and below Glencolumbkille, Columba's Valley, where it opens up to the savage Atlantic breakers. In this valley, on the west coast of Donegal, the memory of the Celtic Church is very much alive.

the most important Columban monastery in Ireland. Indeed, after Iona had been thrice pillaged by the Vikings in 807, Kells became one of the two headquarters of the league of Columban monasteries. With the exception of the cross which is situated in the market square, the other Celtic artefacts at Kells are conveniently situated together. With the exception, that is, of the greatest artefact of all. The Columban monastery at Kells produced the well-known Book of Kells (now in Trinity College, Dublin), an illuminated manuscript of the Four Gospels in Latin.

It struck us outside St. Columba's oratory, some few hundred yards away from the church grounds. Summer dusk was already approaching and, before nightfall, we had an appointment at Athlone, a hundred miles west. 'And miles to go before we sleep! And miles to go before we sleep!' chortled Buffy.

As the Peugeot rattled over the winding miles, we rehearsed what we had learned in this land of saints and scholars and marvelled that it was only forty-eight hours since we had landed there and, on the instant, fallen prey to its powerful spell.

CHAPTER SIX

FROM GLENDALOUGH TO GALWAY BAY

As WE HURTLED towards Athlone cumulus clouds, moments ago innocuous in the mid-summer twilight, were boiling up a storm. A shunt of thunder heralded the bash of rain against windscreen. The road was awash, the car causing a tidal wave on either side.

At Mullingar the lightning stabbed at what looked like a vast Italian cathedral. Entering Athlone, the storm unabated, lightning illuminated another such edifice. The electrified darkness gave them dramatic perspective. In the sane light of day Ralph Byrne's creations (1936-38) appeared incongruous graftings on to these essentially Irish cities.

Crossing the bridge at Athlone, and near journey's end, the electrified darkness also made it possible to recapture a past of battles fought on that spot from the days of the High Kings, through Cromwell, to William of Orange.

Rain-sodden and, at last, at journey's end, we came to anchor abaft the inevitable Irish landlady; 'Well now, it's what God pours through the hole in the sky that puts the emerald into Ireland . . . .'

Celtic Kildare

Athlone had a different aspect under morning sunshine. But the long haul of the previous day had taken its toll on Buffy. When I entered his room he opened one eye and gave me to understand that he received no uplift from the azure firmament and felt that the heartiness of the birds outside the window was, in the circumstances, overdone and in dubious taste.

However, such are the restorative properties of a good Irish breakfast, that before 9am Buffy Trumpton had the map spread out on the table and was contemplating the Wicklow Mountains with his customary moderate enthusiasm.

We made for County Kildare. We resisted the Hill of Allen — home of the hero of Celtic legend, Fionn MacCool — together with great houses like Castletown and great colleges like Maynooth, fetching up in the centre of Kildare itself. Its small cathedral reminded us of St. David's in Wales and was of equally ancient foundation. First established in 480 it is dedicated to St. Brigid 'a prophetess of Christ, the Queen of the South, the Mary of Gael': another Celtic saint. Founded by Brigid, it is clear from seventh-century descriptions that the cathedral — then the principal church of the Kingdom of Leinster — was once far grander than it is now. The presence of the inevitable Round Tower indicates that, even this far inland, precautions against Viking marauders were still necessary.

Of equal importance for the Celtic Church is the site of Old Kilcullen. Three of its carved Celtic crosses date from the eighth century, and the settlement itself was founded by St. Patrick. Among its early bishops was Mac Tail who died in 549. A Round Tower, partially destroyed when it was used as a stronghold in the Wolfe Tone rebellion of 1798, together with traces of the nave and chancel of a Romanesque church, survive.

Glendalough

We tunnelled miles of all-but-covered-over lanes before reaching the broad, open lands affording an uninterrupted view of the Wicklow Mountains. Here, as elsewhere in Ireland, everything appeared in rich, varying shades of green. Rarely did another colour break into the soothing harmony. Everywhere the land was struggling and heaving with the rich green of life given by the rains.

As we covered the undulating foothills, against the distant wall of mountain, we caught sight of great birds of prey riding the thermals. Before long, in second, then bottom gear, we were struggling up the mountain road that snakes through the pass to the north of the Wicklow Gap. To the south was the sheer drop that gave us the bird's eye view and, at the same time, made it perilous to enjoy it for more than fleeting glimpses at a time.

In the depths below, the verdure was less lush and, as we climbed, both sides of the steep valley were covered with the bright yellow of gorse. We turned a tight bend and the whole grandeur of Glendalough broke upon the eye.

Here was a different land, a narrow valley caught up in the Wicklow Mountains, hemmed in and around by murmurous woods. Nestled deep in the green depths we caught sight of quaint ecclesiastical architecture and Celtic crosses.

As we descended towards the Heritage Centre, the sun was shining and the air was quiveringly transparent. Beyond the Centre were narrow, fast rivers flowing into two lakes and, beyond, seas of bluebells washed around the shores of the green land.

Visits to Glendalough should begin at the Heritage Centre. The great monastic settlement in Glendalough, we learned, dated from the sixth century and reflected the strength of Christianity and learning in Ireland when the rest of Europe lay under the pall of the 'Dark Ages'.

We began with an audio-visual presentation. The Celtic missionaries, like the Latins after them, the voice intoned, found the grandest settings for their monastic settlements. St. Kevin who chose this great glen with high, thickly-pined mountains on either side, belonged to the same generation as St. Columba.

St. Columba, we learned, had been born at Lough Gartan, Donegal. He had studied under Finian of

Clonard. Columba had belonged to the family of the High Kings and had founded monasteries in many parts of Ireland including those at Derry, Durrow and in Glencolumbkille.

In 563 Columba had been obliged to flee to Scotland following his refusal to return a copy he had made of Finian's *Psalter*. With a few friends he had crossed the narrow seas in a coracle and landed on Iona. From Iona he and his missionaries had converted the Picts to Christianity, founding centres all over Scotland. Prior to his death in 597 his missionaries had spread the Gospel of Christ to northern Britain . . . .

The brilliantly-presented audio-visual display demonstrated how, from places like Glendalough and Armagh in Ireland, and subsequently Iona and Dunkeld in Scotland, the Celtic missionaries had spread the Gospel to Lindisfarne, Jarrow, Durham, Whitby, Ripon, York, the Yeo Valley, Glastonbury and Cornwall (England); to Cambrai, Meaux and Fontaine (France); to Aachen, Köln, Nürnberg and Mainz (Germany); and even to as far afield as Vienna, Verona and Fiesole.

There are nature trails galore up and around the lakes, forests and mountains of Glendalough. These are best tackled in the daytime with the aid of the specially-prepared guide book. Those of an adventurous spirit might, however, like Buffy and some American friends, decide to tackle one of the mountain paths in the moonlight. With the aid of a bright torch they snaked their way up the mountain path and, atop a ridge, had a bit of a fright. The beams of the torch caught weird shapes and a dozen sets of red, frightening eyes. Had they begun to run back down the path at that point, they might have spread the story that this National Park contained *super*natural phenomena! However, as their eyes became acclimatized, they realized that they were looking into the startled faces of a dozen or so lofty-antlered red stags . . . .

From the Heritage Centre we followed the rhododendron-banked silver river to the monastic site. In the process of so doing we met an assortment of friendly Americans. In the ten minutes or so in which the rain came down in stair-rods, sheltering together we were able to share our impressions.

The rain over, the sun back, we went in search of Glendalough's 'seven churches'. Inside the Heritage Centre had been a model of the monastic settlement to scale. This enabled us to visualize what to look for, and where.

Most of the Celtic buildings have been reconstructed, using original materials as far as possible, by the Board of Works.

We had sheltered from the rain in St. Kevin's Hermitage. Making for the Upper Lake we discovered the tiny Reefert church where, according to tradition, the local kings were buried. Certainly in the adjoining cemetery there are many ancient stone crosses and gravestones, together with the remains of St. Kevin's Cell, a beehive hut.

The earliest monastic sites, on the south side of the Upper Lake, can only be approached by boats. Of these, one is a cave where St. Kevin is believed to have lived, and the other is Templenaskellig, the remains of a large rectangular church.

In the vicinity of the Round Tower, reconstructed from the original stones, are more ancient Celtic crosses, the square tower of St. Mary's church and the ruins of a cathedral dedicated to St. Peter and St. Paul.

No one is asserting that *all* the buildings by any means originate from Celtic times. However, the most 'recent' of the structures predates the twelfth century.

Glendalough, in the subtlest possible way, caters for tourists. However, thick tree cover prevents the hotels, restaurants and craft shops from obtruding.

As we set off for our overnight billet near Rathdrum we concluded that even a week of exploration would not do justice to Glendalough.

Rathdrum was to prove the end of a perfect day. The evening sun was warm as we took an after-dinner walk with our fellow 'inmates' (as Buffy called the other guests). Again we were impressed by the intensity of the greens. Over the distant peaks we watched the sun go down into a gulf of purple. It was difficult to see why Charles Stuart Parnell, 'The Uncrowned King of Ireland', should have been so eager to forsake his home at Avondale House on the edge of Rathdrum for the society of Kitty O'Shea, 'that English woman'.

The road to Galway

In the course of the daylong drive to Galway we took in Durrow in County Laois, and found the inhabitants of this beautiful town strangely unaware of their Columban associations.

We also dropped in at Aghaboe where St. Cainneach, a companion of Columba who was to follow him to Scotland, founded a monastery around 577. The ruins of Aghaboe abbey have been lovingly restored and its story preserved for all to read.

Having driven through fifty miles of flat, somewhat unremarkable terrain, we arrived in Galway at 4.30 and booked into our guest house. We had been assured that our rooms would overlook the 'Galway Bay' of song and story. And so they did. But the bay was a bit of a disappointment. It represents a vast expanse of water chiefly surrounded by flat land. Only in the distance, to the south-west, could we catch sight of misty mountains. From these mountains, we were assured, was the only angle from which Buffy Trumpton could realize his ambition of watching 'the sun go down on Galway bay'.

Galway is one of Ireland's most rapidly-expanding cities. It is one of the computer capitals of Europe and has a cosmopolitan population. It is also an educational centre. The high point of our stay: a dinner in an ancient restaurant on Galway central square reminiscent of Buffy's much-missed club in Pall Mall.

CHAPTER SEVEN

COLUMBA'S LAND AND PATRICK'S MOUNTAINS

WITH THE MELTING of the last of the twilight there grew a kind of expectancy, a tension. Suddenly a gale hit the house and shook all the windows. It came off the Atlantic. All night the rain lashed the bedroom windows. But it had gone by breakfast. On the edge of Galway Bay we could see the shapes of trees and roofs from which streamers of mist trailed down like broken waves pouring from rocks.

The garrulous Americans with whom we shared breakfast wanted to talk about the gale. But our wonderful Irish landlady professed she had not heard it. 'Ireland would be a wonderful place if you could roof it,' said she. 'If we could ship all our rain to the Arabs and if they could ship all their oil to us we should be happy.'

Knock and Croagh Patrick

The real beauty of Galway country is in the mountains, lakes and inlets to the north-west: Connemara. We found, all unexpectedly, a huge Christ-figure with arms outstretched over lough and sea. And, in a neighbouring village, shared a meal with a dozen old women who, with a reverent, whispering sadness, prepared us for disappointment at Knock. They told us that, in 1879, two young women claimed to have seen and talked to the Virgin Mary.

After a decade or so of hype, Knock, a small town in

County Mayo, now rivals Lourdes as a place for pilgrimage. It has the largest car park we had ever seen and, despite the proximity of Shannon, it is building its own international airport. Purpose-built shops and kiosks sell curios and holy water in plastic containers of four sizes.

The vast concreted area surrounding the basilicas is well signposted. People were muttering prayers as they approached the great glass chapel attached to the old church for a healing service at 11am. Inside we could see, in white plaster, a great sculpture of Mary meeting the young women at Knock. The bells calling the sick and lame for healing were pre-recorded and broadcast from speakers atop the old church tower.

Visitors to Knock are now counted in millions per year. So many, in fact, that a vast new basilica has had to be erected. In the centre of the concreted acres before it, was a great concrete cross. Around it are many facilities for mass to be celebrated outdoors, each with its own concrete altar and, behind, three crosses with three life-sized figures writhing upon them.

—o—

The challenge of Croagh Patrick, rising 2,510 feet out of Clew Bay, was just what the doctor ordered. No one tried to sell us holy water as, stiffening the sinews and summoning up the blood, we set out to climb Ireland's Holy Mountain. Buffy, who had been all for the climb, decided he would spend the next few hours in a conveniently-placed restaurant. Hence I was accompanied by an American friend we had picked up in Galway.

On this mountain Patrick is said to have fasted for forty days. But our companions made this a lighthearted pilgrimage. All to the good, especially when we reached the upper cone of the mountain and discovered it to be bare scree. There were fitter, faster climbers than we were, but we did our best to keep up, and on reaching the ruins of 'Patrick's Church' we had prayer. More prayers were said at 'Patrick's Bed', a heap of stones near a modern chapel. Although we decided to forego the customary seven circuits round the summit we nevertheless broke no records in either our ascent or descent of Croagh Patrick.

Having parted unwillingly from our trans-Atlantic friend, bed and board were now a pressing priority.

Donegal: Columba's land

We set out early on the long drive to Glencolumbkille, Donegal. Passing bays impaled by the last tides of the Atlantic, we motored on until we reached Drumcliffe. Even without the historical associations, the mighty green mountain wall running east-west, and the dramatic scenery surrounding, would have made us want to pause here. Drumcliffe is W. B. Yeats country. He is buried in the shade of the imposing edifice of the Church of Ireland.

More importantly, we were in Columba country. The main road slices through a monastic site, partially excavated, which represents a settlement established by St. Columba himself. Two Celtic crosses have been carted off to the National Museum in Dublin. But one sculpted high cross, dating from the ninth century, remains, as does the stump of a Round Tower.

After Drumcliffe we had no scheduled stops before Glencolumbkille. However, we had counted without the spectacular coastal scenery at Bundoran, one of Ireland's most popular seaside resorts. By now the sun shone from a cloudless sky. But the good-weather message had yet to get through to the westerly gale, and the sea was being whipped up to a frenzy. Mountainous, white-capped Atlantic breakers were smashing against the rocks with a thunder that could be heard throughout the resort. The scene must have been unusual even for the local populace. Everywhere eyes were turned west to watch the mighty power of the sea.

Donegal is mountainous. As we turned west out of Donegal town along the coastal road, we began a difficult but breathtakingly beautiful drive. It was to take us along roads perched perilously on mountain ledges but winding inexorably towards Columba's valley.

When we reached Glencolumbkille, near the extreme westerly point of Donegal, the sea had not lost its force. Skies were bright, but we imagined this remote place of thatched dwellings as it turned its face to *winter* gales . . . .

There was only one place in Glencolumbkille to eat, so we ate there. And there was only one place to stay, so we stayed there.

Glencolumbkille, Columba's valley, begins high and narrow in the green Donegal mountains. It then broadens gradually, affording rich peat lands. The settlement is where the valley is broad with mountain ridges to north and south and a barrier of sand and rock to keep out the fury of the ocean.

On the south side of the valley mouth is the Folk Village, a collection of thatched cottages each representing, in a sort of time capsule, life as it would have been in some bygone century. Scenery notwithstanding, the soil is poor in Columba's valley and, century by century, life has been hard. Only in the last quarter century, through the efforts of the energetic Father MacDyer, has a co-operative movement been founded to take advantage of the region's assets. Living standards are now much higher. All over the valley there is evidence of renovation and newly-thatched cottages.

In the poor, stony soil of this valley Columba established a monastic settlement. On St. Columba's day (9 June) there is a 5-kilometre pilgrimage around the Stations of the Cross. Since these highlight many of the ancient sites in the valley we followed the pilgrims' route. It begins at the stone age court-grave in the cemetery of the Protestant Church and takes in the dry-stone Columba's chapel with its ring enclosure, the chapel of Columba's Bed, Columba's well, the Pilgrimage Garden and a number of cross-carved pillars.

The valley was basking in sunshine as we took the road up mountain to Ardara. In this valley, more than anywhere else in Ireland, the distant past had seemed close at hand and our imaginations had recaptured the ascetic life of the ancient Irish saints. Only by promising ourselves that we would one day return, could we bear to leave.

Now we were in search of Lough Gartan amid the mountainous country of Donegal. This had been Columba's birthplace (*circa* 521) and was, we knew, a place of great beauty. It was not difficult to spot it on the map, but finding it along endless, narrow, winding mountainous roads was quite another proposition.

Gartan is situated between two beautiful lakes where tree-covered hills run down to the water's edge. The Heritage Centre, built in stone with a Round Tower to resemble an ancient Irish church, is the best place to begin.

A flagstone in the Glenveagh Estate is reputed to mark Columba's birthplace. Columba was, we learned, of royal blood and was educated in the great monastic schools of Moville (Donegal) and Clonard (County Meath).

Near the village of Churchill on Lough Gartan is the early sixteenth-century St. Columba's chapel, covering the remains of a sixth-century altar and the ruins of an ancient abbey.

From Lough Gartan the road to Columba's first monastery — at Derry — was easy to find. We had time to enjoy something of the beauties of Lough Foyle before striking south through the superior roads of Ulster for our night's stay in a farm near Dungannon.

Patrick's country

All parts of Ireland, of course, lay claim to St. Patrick, but it is possible that the south-eastern corner of Ulster has the closest associations.

The existence of well-maintained dual-carriageways in Ulster meant that travel was a great deal faster. Hence, despite competing with the rush-hour traffic pouring into Belfast, we reached Bangor, where Belfast Lough becomes the Irish Sea, before the town was fully awake.

Perhaps the most interesting feature at the Heritage Centre was a model of the town and religious settlement as it would have been at the time of St. Comgall, a disciple of St. Columba. St. Comgall founded the monastic settlement *circa* 555 but, because of its accessibility from the sea, it suffered more than most from the ravages of the Vikings.

The great saints and scholars of the sixth century and after were trained at Bangor. However, the repeated attacks of the Vikings wiped out the settlement for a period of centuries. In 1124, however, St. Malachy revived and rebuilt the monastery. Bangor Castle, next to the Heritage Centre, and Bangor Abbey church, west of Castle Park, are the sites of historical interest here.

But we were in search of St. Patrick. Having enjoyed the scenic route to the east of Strangford Lough and having waited for a local wedding party, we crossed the narrow sea at Portaferry.

We had no clear idea what we were looking for as we wound our way towards the village of Saul. No one had prepared us for what caught our eye at the turn of the road. In the distance we saw a great monolith, a statue of some sort, dominating the skyline. After some exploration and a few enquiries we found our way to an imposing gate entrance. Behind the gate a wide green, sloping sharply up mountain, cut a swathe through the forest. It was going to be another of those occasions for stiffening the sinews and summoning up the blood. Here was a prospect Buffy did not relish. But muttering something about 'if it were done when 'tis done, then 'twere well it were done quickly', he began the stiff ascent, stopping only occasionally for a breather.

This was Patrick's second mountain. Near the top, where the final Station of the Cross had been left behind, was a sculptured crucifixion scene, with a stone altar before it. On the pinnacle of the mountain was the great statue of St. Patrick himself, the focus of many a pilgrimage. In every direction we could see for miles. There were loughs and seas, rolling grasslands and patchworked fields, two or three churches, tiny from this altitude, and in the distance, the shape of Downpatrick where the great saint was buried.

Having completed the descent and motored through the village of Saul we visited St. Patrick's Memorial Church. Built in the idiom of the ancient places of worship, complete with Round Tower, this Protestant church makes the claim to have been built on the site of the first Christian church in Ireland built on land granted to St. Patrick in AD432 and thus to be 'the most ancient ecclesiastical site in this land, the cradle of Irish Christianity'.

Downpatrick Cathedral is an experience not to be missed, whether or not one believes the claims of twelfth-century King John de Courcy that the remains of St. Patrick, St. Columba and St. Brigid were interred beneath its grounds. The great stone in the cemetery is believed to cover the tomb of St. Patrick. Regardless of its authenticity or otherwise, almost everyone seems to believe that St. Patrick founded a church inside Rath Celtchair, a hill fort, part of whose rampart is traceable south-west of the cathedral. The remains of a monastery, revitalized by St. Malachy, are certainly there to be examined. Outside the east end of the cathedral is a ninth-century High Cross which formerly stood at the centre of the town.

The day was waning as we sped to Armagh, the ancient ecclesiastical capital of the British Isles, where we were to spend our last weekend in the Emerald Isle.

Armagh

The fame of Armagh rests on its choice by St. Patrick to be the site of his principal church (*circa* 445). Certainly from the early eighth century the bishop-abbots of Armagh, as heirs of St. Patrick, claimed to be primates over the whole Irish Church.

Armagh, we discovered, was built around three hills. On one of these hills is the imposing Roman Catholic cathedral built in the last century.

On another hill is the ancient Protestant (Church of Ireland) cathedral of St. Patrick. This is generally accepted to have been built on the site of St. Patrick's ancient church and to have been the venue for many synods. The present squat building has been much altered, but has a medieval core.

On the third hill is the Armagh Observatory, the world's oldest, and celebrating its two-hundredth anniversary when we called in. Dutchman Dr. Mart de Groot, the chief of the observatory, graciously conducted us around this high-tech scientific centre founded by an eighteenth-century bishop. Even more graciously he invited us to spend the weekend with him and his family at his home outside of the city.

Hence it was after a well-rested weekend in the company of this world-renowned astronomer and his delightful family that we motored across country towards Larne and the Sealink ferry for Stranraer.

It was late evening when we caught a glimpse of the coast of Scotland made ruddy by the reflection of a blood-red sunset. Though homesick for Ireland, we wondered what adventures were in store for us as we pilgrimaged through this other proud kingdom.

CHAPTER EIGHT

FROM GALLOWAY TO IONA

STRANRAER AT FIRST light. Everything looked barnacled and deathly quiet. The town was submerged by a greenish sunlight and the tangy scents of the sea.

But the sun rose and waxed strong. We were not to know, as the Peugeot filed out of town behind a convoy of trucks from the morning ferry, that the sun was asserting an ascendency that morning that it would maintain all summer long.

A saint before Patrick

We were making for Whithorn on the Wigtown peninsula in search of St. Ninian. First, there is Whithorn itself, where the excavations of a monastery are to be found. Second, there is Isle of Whithorn on the coast, where St. Ninian's chapel is located. Third, there is Ninian's cave on the rocky coast to the west of the peninsula.

Passing through the archway that leads off Whithorn's main street we found ourselves on one of the oldest Christian settlements in Britain. A little way off were the ruins of a medieval priory dating from the days when Whithorn was a university city.

'Hold on! I'm fogged!' said Buffy Trumpton. 'I thought old Patrick came first. You know, our first missionary and all that. Who was this Ninian fellow?'

I explained that there had probably been Christians in Ireland *before* Patrick but that he was Christ's first really great champion. And that there had certainly been

Christians in Britain before Columba, among them Roman legionaries.

By now Buffy was reading a Tourist Information board and looking even more confused. ' "Ninian was born in the second half of the fourth century," ' he read. 'Doesn't that mean some time between AD 350 and 400?'

'Affirmative,' I replied.

'Right then,' barged Buffy, 'I told you so. Ninian had his foot in the door before Patrick.'

He read further down the information board and felt sure he had run across new historic truth and that I was confounded. 'See here!' said he, wagging the forefinger. '*You* said that Patrick, Columba and that Celtic crew had different beliefs from the Roman lot . . . .'

I confirmed that such was the case.

' . . . It says here that Ninian caught Christianity on visits to Rome and Gaul and that it was *Roman* Christianity that he taught here.'

'Time to back up,' said I, inviting him to occupy a bench doubtless provided by the locals for the historically confused.

I told him that what information we had about Ninian came from three sources. First, Bede's *A History of the English Church and People* (written three centuries after Ninian's death). Second, an eighth-century Latin poem of great length compiled by a monk called Alcuin (735-804). Third, a sort of biography of Ninian by Reginald of Durham who had visited Whithorn in 1164.

Buffy was beginning to look drowsy. 'Any sensible selection committee would choose *you* to bore for England!' he grumbled. But I bored on.

From the three available sources it was clear, I told him, that Ninian had visited Martin of Tours in Gaul, but that only one of the three sources mentioned a trip to Rome. It was, however, clear that Ninian had brought Christianity back to Galloway and that, at so early a period, it was likely to have been more 'Celtic' than 'Roman'.

Buffy came to with a start. 'Didn't you say that Patrick was born in Galloway or Dumbarton or the Solway Firth or somewhere? Couldn't he have learned what he knew from Ninian?'

I congratulated him on spotting that the life-spans of Ninian and Patrick overlapped, and conceded that, since available sources indicated that Ninian had established a college in Whithorn, Patrick was believed by some to have been tutored there. (To avoid a breakdown of diplomatic relations, I omitted to mention that the legend that Patrick was born in the Galloway region may well have been invented to explain his initial contact with Christianity — through Ninian — and that one school of thought still believed that Patrick was born in Wales. . . .)

But Buffy was running up the white flag from sheer impatience. 'All right. Let's have the facts,' he demanded.

From the three historical sources and the archaeological evidence he had just seen, I told him, it was clear that a man called Ninian had been converted to Christianity at Tours and returned to Whithorn to preach the Gospel. At Whithorn he had founded a monastery. Here he had trained missionaries who had evangelized the Picts who lived between the Clyde and the Solway Firth. He had died circa 432. Among his successors had been St. Mungo who, about 543, had built the first church in what is now Glasgow and to whom Glasgow Cathedral is dedicated.

We took one last look at the excavations of Ninian's monastery and at the ruins of the twelfth-century priory. Then we took the road to Isle of Whithorn and St. Ninian's chapel, before driving five miles back up the peninsula. Here we noticed a sign marked 'St. Ninian's Cave' and walked along the grassy path that leads to the cliffs. With some difficulty we climbed up to and into Ninian's Cave. Even on a hot summer day it was dank and solitary. In later centuries others, like Ninian, had used this cave as a place of retreat. Using a torch

66

Buffy was excited to find crosses cut into the walls of the cave.

Within the hour we were on the A74 heading for Glasgow. We took a look at St. Mungo's cathedral before turning in at the Queen's Hotel, overlooking the park.

I recall sharing some of Trumpton's frustrations. Did Ninian belong to the Celtic or to the Roman tradition? And wasn't it by far the simplest explanation of the whole collection of legends that Patrick learned his creed from Ninian? Or was it a question of creed? Perhaps both Ninian and Patrick had first experienced Christianity in Gaul and had chosen to interpret it in different ways? Did distance more than anything else explain the differences between Celtic and Roman Christianity?

Tomorrow we would be making for Oban and, from thence, to Iona. Here perhaps we would find the firmer footing of history.

The road from Iona

The sun was hot and the car windows down as we passed Loch Lomond and took the road to Crianlarich. We were all but cooked when we arrived in Oban and searched its maze of tiered streets for our guest house. It was high up in the half-basin of the steep-sloped town, just below McCaig's Folly. At the quayside we booked the Caledonian McBrayne 'Holy Isle' cruise for the next day. From my bedroom I later looked out on the great island ferries coming and going in the harbour, wondered what a tall sailing vessel was doing there, watched a glorious sunset behind Kerrera and the mountains of Mull, and asked myself if this was not the greatest sight of all.

By 9.30 next day we were aboard one of the larger ferries for the full day cruise of the islands. A palaver of seagulls followed as we sailed past the many-coloured, single-storeyed houses in the half-round of Tobermory harbour on Mull. We dropped anchor off Staffa and looked at the curious rock formations that inspired 'Fingal's Cave' by Mendelssohn (which Buffy proceeded to whistle).

After lunch on board we sailed into the Sound of Iona. The size of the vessel made it necessary for the 200 or so passengers to be put ashore by way of the small boat that serves as a ferry between Mull and Iona. Since there was only one such boat, the operation took some time.

The pier is in Martyr's Bay where sixty-eight monks were slaughtered by Viking marauders in 806.

The first ruins we encountered were those of a Benedictine Nunnery. Not far away was Iona Abbey. In front of the west door of the abbey/cathedral was the beautifully decorated St. Martin's cross which, though in an excellent state of preservation, dates from the ninth century.

But Buffy was keen to pursue the Columba connection. And so was I. Hence, having spent a quiet hour examining the cathedral, we headed for the southern tip of the island to find Columba's Bay and the Port of the Coracle. (Once there, Buffy expressed as a certainty that we would never get back to the pier in time for the homeward ferry.)

In that bay St. Columba and his friends had landed in 563.

Columba was the great-grandson of Conall who, though himself a son of Ireland's first High King, was among the thousands of Irish baptized by Patrick. With a strong claim through his mother Eithne it is likely that Columba gave up a throne for the banner of Christ.

Columba was 41 when, with twelve friends, he crossed the Irish Channel in coracles of wicker and hide to take the Gospel to Britain. On the voyage north they landed briefly in Argyle, decided against settling on the islands of Jura and Colonsay, making for Iona. Having landed there they built a Celtic monastery very near to where the present-day abbey is situated.

King Connel from Dunadd gave Iona to Columba as a missionary base. Soon he and the original twelve were joined by scores, perhaps hundreds of missionaries from Ireland.

But Iona's monasteries and abbeys were intended as

a centre of operations, not a retreat. From there Columba, in the words of Bede, 'converted the nation to the faith of Christ by preaching and example'.

However, for reliable information about Columba we do not have to rely on Bede or on the odd poem here and ballad there. Our knowledge of Columba's life comes from Cummine, Abbot of Iona from 657 to 669, who wrote Columba's biography, and Adomnan, who became Abbot to the Iona community in 679. Cummine had known Columba. Even Adomnan was writing within eighty years of Columba's death.

Columba began his missionary endeavours with the neighbouring Picts, and the mainland bay where he landed — near the road from Oban to Glencoe — is still called Columba's Bay. His aim was to reach the court of King Brude at Inverness by way of the Great Glen. Doubtless Columba was aware of the insecurity of having Iona by the gift of an Irish king. Much of Columba's journey to Brude's palace would have been made in light boats, which could be carried overland between the lochs. Brude was converted to Christianity in 565 and confirmed Columba's right to Iona.

With the support of King Brude it would appear that Columba's missionaries preached the faith along the north-east coast of Scotland from the site of Inverness to the Orkneys. Columba himself would appear to have made a number of sea journeys along the north-west coast of Scotland; a monastery was established on Skye. In 580, when he was over 60, he is said to have travelled with his disciple Drostan into what we now know as Aberdeenshire. Before Columba's death in June 597 a thriving religious centre under his patronage existed at Dunkeld, north of present-day Perth.

It has often been observed that, had the Church adhered to the beliefs and practices of Columba's Celts, a Reformation would have been unnecessary. Bede believed that the disparity between the Celtic and Roman Churches arose because the former 'dwelt beyond the reach of the degrees of synods' and 'could learn only those things contained in the writings of the prophets, the evangelists and the apostles'.

Many twentieth-century scholars have researched the nature of the differences between Rome and the Celts. The most detailed research has been undertaken by Dr. Leslie Hardinge, presented as a PhD dissertation for the University of London and published as *The Celtic Church in Britain* (SPCK 1972). Buffy's fears notwithstanding, we *did* catch the homeward ferry and, before doing so, bought a copy of Dr. Hardinge's book from the nearby bookshop.

According to Hardinge the Celtic Church ✻ believed in the Bible as the only foundation for faith; ✻ found the idea of an ever-burning hell unbiblical, associated it with heathenism and rejected it; ✻ preached that man was saved 'not by the merits of his deeds' but by the unmerited favour of Jesus Christ; ✻ believed in 'Christ the Most High coming down from heaven' (Columba's words), the second advent; ✻ believed in baptism by immersion; ✻ believed in the Ten Commandments as 'Christ's Law' (Columba's words) from whence came the knowledge of sin.

—o—

Before sailing into the Firth of Lorn towards Oban, all on board were aware of an apocalyptic sunset over the western seas. Sky and ocean were alive, running with immense streams of flame. Then, as the sun went down, it seemed to drag the whole sky with it like the shreds of a burning curtain, leaving rags of bright water that went on smouldering.

CHAPTER NINE

REFORMATION SCOTLAND

WHEN BUFFY TRUMPTON first told me that we *must*, simply *must* explore the rest of Scotland from his aunt's place near Perth, I didn't know quite what to expect.

As we chugged up the hill road off the A85 the temperature of my feet dropped sharply, nor did it rise appreciably when we hove up abaft what I had always thought of as a typical Scottish 'but and ben'.

With a 'Pip-pip, old ancestor', Buffy bounded through the door and had the introductions over in a trice. In no time we were warmed through with Scottish hospitality and filled to the earlobes with Scottish provender. Upon inspection, our base of operations turned out to be two 'but and bens' welded into one and fitted with double glazing and every modern convenience.

Buffy's female relatives, mother and daughter, proved an extrovert little wench with an excellent line in humour and a most charming daughter with a lively touch on the piano. Buffy's male relative had the cure of one of those congregations of Scottish souls who believe that they are best served by keeping the clergy in penury. A mine of information about battles in which the Scots . . . er . . . had the advantage over the English (Bannockburn a speciality), he was to prove beyond value in planning out our itineraries. I had only one thing against this impoverished man of the clorth: he drove and expected us to ride in a bright orange, four-wheeled contraption of great antiquity which he called 'car', the chassis of which was quite evidently coming adrift from the body.

Filled with fodder we puffed and sweated our way up the hill behind the manse. I had not heard of Kinnoul Hill and hence was quite unprepared for the vista from the top. With a tower-like folly for foreground we looked east to a commanding view of the Tay Valley, a castle nestling in thick forest below us. Just west we had a near-aerial view of a spaghetti junction and, beyond it, Perth.

Buffy's relatives beamed proprietorially at my drop-jawed wonderment. 'The best view in Scotland,' said the short female relative. 'You speak an imperial quart,' affirmed Buffy.

Before set of sun we had tangled with that spaghetti junction, crossed the Tay, visited the ancient palace of the Scottish kings at Falkland, and seen Kirk of St. Bride, Abernethy, founded by the Celtic missionaries in AD457 and boasting one of only two Irish Round Towers to be found in Scotland.

The Royal Mile

Next morning we took on Edinburgh at rush hour and, by a miracle, found a place to park. The remainder of the day was spent on the Royal Mile in this most grand of British capitals.

The Royal Mile is the name Edinburgh gives to a straight, cobble-stoned thoroughfare that descends gently from the castle, perched high on its rock, eastward to the Palace of Holyrood House at the bottom of the hill. This one street, with its shops and its tall grey tenements, forms the backbone of historic Edinburgh.

Greyfriars

On either side of the Royal Mile are the ribs of the old town. Among these, through an arch, we found Greyfriars church. Here tourist attention centres around 'Greyfriars Bobby', the heroic little dog whose story is better known than that of John Knox. Bobby's tomb is certainly a great deal more dignified than that of Knox and, even as we watched, Bobby's statue was cuddled by children from the four corners of the earth. In Greyfriars churchyard, in addition to Bobby's tomb, is the grave of his master which he guarded for fourteen years.

But the church itself was locked up and scaffolding clambered one of its blackened flanks. I had quite given up my ambition to savour this historic kirk when I heard Buffy's aunt addressing commands to a youth perched high on the scaffolding and playing Radio 3 on his ghetto-blaster. This youth was summoned to earth and bidden to produce a key.

It was in Greyfriars church that the Covenant was signed. Adjacent to the church we found the gaol where the Covenanters were imprisoned. And, in the churchyard, the ornate tomb of the judge who passed sentence on them.

However, to understand the significance of the Covenant and the 'Killing Times', we need first to go downhill to the palace of Holyrood House.

Holyrood

Holyrood Palace was first founded by King David I (1124-53), the son of Malcolm and Margaret who rendered themselves so unpopular by campaigning against the distinctive beliefs and practices of the Celtic Church, and bringing Scottish Christians into line with the Roman Church.

Following the example of his mother, King David sought to consolidate Roman control in Scotland by fostering a network of cathedrals, parish churches and religious houses. Holyrood Palace was built by the side of one such religious house, the ruins of which remain, and was named after what was thought to be a fragment of Christ's cross (rood means cross) which had been presented to David's mother, Margaret.

Holyrood is one of the most ancient of the residences still occupied by the royal family of the United Kingdom. It is certainly one of the most photogenic of the royal palaces and no visit to Scotland would be complete without a visit to it and a careful examination of its interior which is open to the public.

It was in the chapel at Holyrood that Mary Queen of Scots married Lord Darnley in 1565, and where their son James VI (later to be James I of England) was born. It was here that Darnley was involved in the brutal murder of the Queen's Italian secretary, David Rizzio, in 1566. And it was at Kirk o' Field, nearby, that Darnley himself was murdered shortly afterwards.

St. Giles

For 500 years and more the skyline of historic Edinburgh has been dominated by a stone tower constructed in the unmistakable shape of a crown. This is the tower of St. Giles situated at about the halfway point in the Royal Mile, which has been the venue of many pivotal events in the religious history of Scotland.

We entered Scotland's High Kirk and thought of the remarkable story.

The first religious house on the site of St. Giles was founded some 1,100 years ago. In 854, monks from the Celtic community on Lindisfarne, off the Northumbrian coast, came farming in the area with the secondary motive of evangelizing the populace. They built a wooden church and placed a cross at the centre. In 1120 the first stone church was built on the site. This first stone church was destroyed by the English armies of King Richard II. King Robert II of Scotland inspired the people of Edinburgh to rebuild their kirk. This time it was to be Gothic in style. However, it was not until 1495, in the illustrious reign of James IV, that the crown steeple was added. As Buffy's clerical relative was loath to admit, James IV was killed by the English at the Battle of Flodden in 1513. It was in the years after the great King's death that St. Giles became crowded with fifty altars and as many gaudy images. This was St. Giles on the eve of the Reformation.

Scotland's Reformation, unlike that of England, was

achieved by people power. The man who, above all others, inspired the people was John Knox.

John Knox

Knox, with many English Calvinists, found himself in exile in Geneva. In 1555 he returned to his native land and found lodgings just down the road, within sight of St. Giles. He travelled all over Scotland before returning to Geneva. Four years later he returned to rouse his native land like a blast of trumpets. He marched into St. Giles with the Lords of the Congregation and the people, and there, in July 1559, he preached a vehement sermon. In the months thereafter the images and the altars were removed. And, during the years 1560 to 1572 when he was minister of St. Giles, there were a great many more dynamic sermons. St. Giles pulpit, the pulpit of John Knox, was the launching point of the Scottish Reformation.

Knox preached his last sermon in St. Giles in 1572, a fortnight before his death. He was buried in what was then the churchyard of St. Giles. Now, to the embarrassment and shame of our Scottish companions, the tarmac of a car-park covers the ancient graveyard. The body of John Knox is under space 44 of the car-park. Peering under the front of a Vauxhall Astra, we found a small plaque to this effect. To give the Scots their due, however, it has to be said that a statue of Knox is to be found a few yards away from the main door of St. Giles.

Mary Queen of Scots came in state to St. Giles to attend the Scottish parliament which met in the west end of the church. As a Roman Catholic she was opposed to everything Knox stood for, but the times were against her. In the burghs and throughout the Lowlands both people and lairds — and some of the nobles — were Protestants. At one meeting of the Estates, Protestantism was declared the official religion of Scotland.

A few yards down the road from St. Giles we found the house of John Knox. A little imagination has made this house a fascinating experience for visitors. In every room, through concealed loudspeakers, can be heard the voices of actors speaking the lines of Knox and of Mary in their frequent exchanges, and of Knox in full flood from the pulpit. The window above the desk of John Knox affords a wonderful view of St. Giles and the Royal Mile.

After his mother's disgrace, and before succeeding Queen Elizabeth I of England, as James I, James VI of Scotland attended St. Giles regularly. The religious conflict in the years of his minority was centred around the question of whether the Church should be governed by bishops. Following his accession in London, James sought to impose on Scotland a replica of the English Church. Among other things, he was determined to force the Protestant nobles to kneel during Communion. This violated the basic principles of the Reformed faith and smacked of Catholicism. When James died in 1625 they were still stubbornly refusing to kneel.

The Covenant

But the liveliest conflict in St. Giles was to take place during the reign of James's son, Charles I.

In 1633 King Charles I came to Scotland, was crowned in Holyrood Abbey, and proceeded to St. Giles, declaring it, for the first time, a cathedral. But he was extremely displeased to discover that the form of worship was very simple. He decided that things must change in this new cathedral.

In 1637 he sent a new Prayer Book to Scotland.

According to the royal decree the new service was to commence in *all* churches beginning with St. Giles. The Dean of Edinburgh was ordered to conduct the service from the new book. As soon as he began, uproar broke out. A local character, Jenny Geddes, is said to have shouted, 'Traitor! Dost thou say mass at my ear?' And, so saying, she threw the stool on which she had been sitting at his head. Wisely, he ducked. There followed a tumult. Many more stools were flung. The service was discontinued.

The upshot was that a petition was put to the King demanding freedom of religion. When the King refused to accept, they signed the National Covenant at Greyfriars.

The conflict over the Covenant developed into an armed battle in which many lost their lives. It was to be another fifty years before Scotland achieved freedom of religion.

The Killing Times

The worst phase of the Covenant Wars was yet to come. It followed the restoration of the Stuarts in 1660. The Prayer Book was imposed on Scotland, bishops were restored and episcopal incumbents installed in the parish churches. Fines were imposed on those who did not attend church and the military were given the job of collecting them. Long-suffering Presbyterian worshippers were roused to revolt, especially in Dumfries and Galloway. The Covenanter army was raised there, later to be mown down by the King's cavalry.

Those who refused to attend the parish churches and met in secret instead, when caught were subjected to the worst kind of atrocities. Off Wigtown, in the Solway Firth, two women, one of 60, the other under 20, were tied to stakes while the military watched them drown slowly as the tide came up. The same atrocity was repeated elsewhere, as when soldiers pushed more women back into the River Nith at Dumfries when they tried to clamber out. Men were simply shot.

Toleration followed the 1688 Revolution.

Dunkeld

In our time at the manse below Kinnoul Hill day merged into day like a series of dissolving dreams. And, each day, so many toothsome delights were served up for our delectation that Buffy Trumpton was almost visibly expanding.

On the day we spent at Dunkeld, fifteen miles north of Perth on the A9, it was warm. The abbey by the Tay was originally founded by Celts from Iona and, after Iona had been raided a score of times by the Vikings, the monks who did not return to Ireland moved to Dunkeld making it the centre of operations for the Celtic Church in Scotland.

Dunkeld is a beautiful town in a beautiful setting sheltered from the winds on all sides by high hills. Half the cathedral church, built over the Celtic site, is in regular use by the Church of Scotland. The other half has been in ruins since the Reformation. In the shadow of great trees and so near to the Tay, Dunkeld Cathedral may well be the most charmingly situated ecclesiastical building in Scotland. But Viking longboats soon found their way to these upper reaches of the Tay, and the Celtic settlers suffered repeated assaults.

Perth

'Whatever you say about the Victorians,' pronounced Buffy, 'there were very few who could be trusted within reach of a trowel and a pile of bricks.'

At Dunkeld was the strong ambience of history. Not so at St. John the Baptist's Kirk, the centre of the religious story in the beautiful city of Perth. Here Victorian renovation and rebuilding rendered one of Scotland's beautiful fifteenth-century churches decidedly mundane.

The beauties of St. John's lie inside.

Following the first return of John Knox to Scotland in 1555 the Regent, Mary of Guise, the Queen Mother, had him tried *in absentia*. His body was condemned to be burned and his soul to be damned. On his second return from Geneva, in April 1559, this sentence was still hanging over him. The Regent, hearing of his return, summoned him to appear for trial at Stirling Castle. Knox and his followers rode past Stirling, making straight for St. John's, Perth. When they entered, mass was being celebrated. Knox marched to the pulpit and, as the townspeople surged in behind him, preached the bold Protestant sermon that unleashed the flood-tide that carried with it monasteries throughout the Lowlands. No one could touch him now.

St. Andrew's

No golf enthusiast will pass up a chance to visit St. Andrews. Buffy had, early on in our stay, edged it on to the agenda. On the day we visited the city, Buffy put in his hours at the links, his female relatives disported themselves on the wide expanse of sand and shallow sea, and the learned cleric and I went off in search of history.

St. Andrews castle and cathedral are both in ruins. However, there is enough on both sites to provide an idea of what vast, imposing structures they once were.

This is especially true of the cathedral. No serious historian now doubts that St. Andrews was originally one of the Celtic settlements. Like St. Giles its link is with the Northumbrian Celts rather than the missionaries from Iona.

The building of the great ecclesiastical house at St. Andrews was, indirectly, as a result of the work of Margaret. Margaret, a Saxon, had fled to Scotland following the Norman conquest and, after a torrid love affair, married King Malcolm of Scotland. The building of a series of Augustinian houses, including St. Andrews, was part of their policy of confounding Celtic Christianity in Scotland. The great cathedral was completed in 1160.

On the eve of the Reformation, St. Andrews was one of the grandest ecclesiastical establishments in the whole of Christendom.

My visit to the castle began with an examination of the initials 'GW' set in the road.

At an early stage in the European Reformation the teachings of Luther had spread to Scotland. To the anger of the Archbishop of St. Andrews, the King's grandson, Patrick Hamilton, began espousing Lutheranism at the university. Hamilton was burned as a heretic in 1528.

'GW' — George Wishart — was another great martyr for the Reformed religion in St. Andrews. Hamilton died with the cry on his lips, 'How long, O God, shall darkness cover this kingdom?' Others, including Wishart, took up the implied challenge. There were more burnings.

Wishart himself was burned in March 1546 on the spot marked by his initials in the road. Cardinal David Beaton watched from a nearby window in the castle (still *in situ*). He and his friends gave every evidence of enjoying the spectacle of a man being strangled and burned for his faith.

On an evening in May of the same year a group of young noblemen and their retainers entered the castle. They were heavily outnumbered. But, by the end of the evening, Cardinal Beaton's corpse was thrown from the same window from which he had witnessed Wishart's burning.

Among Wishart's many disciples was John Knox.

Stirling

On a glorious day when the sun scorched rather than warmed, we bade a fond farewell at Stirling to our Scottish hosts.

The Church of the Holy Rood claims the attention of all visitors. Following the abdication of his mother, Mary Queen of Scots, the infant James VI was hastily crowned there on 29 July 1567. The preacher at his coronation was Knox. On many other occasions the voice of the great reformer reverberated through the ancient kirk.

Until recent years only half the church was in use, the other half having remained in ruins since the Reformation. Now, through extensive and authentic restoration work, the entire building is being brought back to its pristine splendour.

Not far from the great kirk is Stirling's castle, built on a great promontory from which it dominates the Scottish Lowlands. Outside its main gate is the statue of Robert the Bruce and, visible against a mountain back-drop, is the Wallace Monument and, a little further over, the site of the Battle of Bannockburn.

Stirling and Edinburgh castles are closely identified with the secular history of Scotland. Both were built on great outcrops of rock and were, thus, easily defensible. Both castles were favoured residences of successive Scot-

Greyfriars Church,
Edinburgh, where the
Covenant was signed,
adjacent to the gaol
where the
Covenanters were
imprisoned.

The ruins of
Rievaulx, a Cistercian
abbey, in an idyllic,
remote north
Yorkshire valley.

St. Giles, on the Royal Mile, Edinburgh,
viewed from the house of John Knox.
From the pulpit of St. Giles, Knox
thundered his Reformation sermons.

AMAZING GRACE !
HOW SWEET THE SOUND
JOHN NEWTON

Olney, Buckinghamshire, the parish of John Newton, slave captain turned clergyman. In William Cowper's Olney home, preserved as it was when he lived in it, Cowper and Newton composed 'The Olney Hymns'. The greatest of them is celebrated in a window in the parish church.

The ruins of the ancient abbey at Walsingham, north Norfolk. The shrines at Walsingham were the strongest magnet for pilgrims for centuries. Roman Catholic pilgrims continue to visit them in large numbers.

The interior of the 'Bunyan Meeting', Mill Street, Bedford. The stained glass windows of the chapel illustrate scenes from John Bunyan's greatest work, written in Bedford Gaol *Pilgrim's Progress*. Right, Christian reaches Calvary where the burden of guilt rolls from his back.

Near Bedford is the village of Elstow where the great Nonconformist preacher and writer was born and lived.

HE HATH GIVEN ME REST BY HIS SORROW AND LIFE BY HIS DEATH

John Wesley travelled on horseback 6,000 miles a year on the mud roads of eighteenth-century England preaching in the open air. His story begins at the Rectory, Epworth, Lincolnshire (below) and takes in Bristol, West Yorkshire, Cornwall, Tyneside — and the City Road Chapel, London. In front of this chapel is Wesley's statue, behind is his tomb, and by the side is the house which was his home for many years.

Lincoln's magnificent cathedral. In the days before Christmas the steep, cobbled streets that climb up to the cathedral and castle take on the atmosphere of the Middle Ages. For thousands Lincoln's 'Christmas Fayre' is the high point of the season.

St. David's Cathedral. St. Asaph, Llantwit Major and St. David's are the centres of Celtic Christianity in Wales.

Fountains Abbey near Ripon, north Yorkshire, one of the largest religious houses in medieval Christendom, where the Cistercians believed they had found 'a purer paradise'.

tish kings and progressively rebuilt in accordance with changing royal tastes.

Mary Queen of Scots was crowned in the chapel in 1543, escaped from death by fire in the castle in 1561 and witnessed the baptism of her son there in 1566. During the Reformation struggle her mother, Mary of Guise, garrisoned the castle with French troops to defend the monarchy and the Catholic faith.

The castle and its grounds merit a full day's exploration. Visitors are taken by surprise by the lawns and flower-filled gardens.

At first on our long drive home Buffy Trumpton displayed all the verve of a cold rice pudding. Then, somewhere past Carlisle, he suddenly looked up from the book he had been reading, full of pep: 'What about Lindisfarne, and Whitby and Jarrow?' he demanded. 'And why are we going the wrong way?'

CHAPTER TEN

LOW TIDE AT LINDISFARNE

LINDISFARNE, THE HOLY ISLE, is placed precariously between the fury of the North Sea and the bleak, squally north Northumberland coast. Just south of the Scottish border, it is eight miles from Bamburgh, capital of the ancient kingdom of Northumbria.

The Holy Isle is stitched to the mainland by a great hem of sand and tummocky brown turf. Here is felt the salt bitter passion of the sea, its strength, its attack — and its indifference to the fragile land lifeline.

At high tide Lindisfarne is out of reach, visitors' cars marooned on the Slakes, and the island community takes on a different, ageless atmosphere. At low tide tourists have their precarious access, North Sea anger permitting. Across that narrow causeway a howling, persistent wind blows for most of the year. Its savage coldness, the islanders tell you, can all but skin you alive.

Another 'Holy Isle'

It was an overcast day that found our tyres skittering unsteadily over the uneven causeway across the low tide to Lindisfarne. Once on the island itself we followed the narrow road that curves between the wilderness of sand-dunes on the downward leg of the shapeless island — and the bay. Over the dunes was a ground fog like wire wool. The bay and the village settlement on the seaward neck of the island were shrouded in seeping mist.

We abandoned the Peugeot and looked over the weather-swept greys to the castle which, announced

Buffy, was built by Henry VIII against the Scots. 'Looks like a walnut whip,' he pronounced contemptuously.

Where the bay swept out to the seaward promontory on which the inverted cornet of the castle was built, it was lined with upturned boats of various sizes, the larger ones truncated, fitted with doors and used for storage. Only the piled-high lobster baskets gave evidence of a branch of the fishing industry still practised here.

The road to the coastguard station might afford us an opportunity to overview the island sufficiently to receive some conception of its geography. We took this climbing road. The long grass was sea-drenched. Not far below, waves were bursting in a shock of foam against defiant rock.

From one vantage point the village looked green-lit. Immediately below us, between us and the village, were the ruins of the once vast priory of the Holy Isle. A storm was gathering overhead and the scatter of heavy drops urged our steps as we sped down the hill to the ruins. Passing the gaunt statue of St. Aidan, his back to a Celtic cross, we saw a grey curtain of rain was moving swiftly in from the sea to meet us.

We sheltered under the ornamented Norman doorway to the west of the priory and thought of the beginnings of this ancient place . . . .

First the Bible-based Gospel brought by Columba to Iona, that *other* holy isle to the west of Scotland. We thought of Aidan's mission from Iona in 634, thirty-seven years after Columba's death. Having boned up on the subject, Buffy was ready to set Aidan's mission in its historic context. At the time of Aidan's arrival, he told me, Oswald had just made himself king of Northumbria after a victory over Welsh Prince Cadwallader at Heavenfield, near Hadrian's Wall. Oswald, already under Christian influence, welcomed the Celtic missionary and asked him to appeal to Iona for more teachers for his people.

Aidan had chosen Lindisfarne as his headquarters because it had reminded him of Iona and because it was near the Northumbrian capital of Bamburgh.

Aidan and Cuthbert

In an uncertain lull between downpours, we ran over to a bookshop in the village. Here there was no shortage of good histories of the island community. We bought one each and, having booked in to the Christian retreat centre, we spent the rainy evening in the lounge reading them.

From Aidan's headquarters on Lindisfarne — no more than a collection of primitive huts and a small oratory — the whole of Northumbria was evangelized. Aidan was the first of sixteen bishops of Lindisfarne. Perhaps the most famous of the sixteen was Cuthbert who became Bishop in 685. When he died, two years later, his body was laid in a stone coffin.

Cuthbert's fame brought many pilgrims to the Holy Isle and, in 698, his body was exhumed and placed in a wooden coffin, still preserved at Durham. When the coffin was opened in 1104 a sixth-century manuscript of St. John's gospel was discovered, doubtless having belonged to St. Cuthbert himself. The leather covering, with its Celtic ornamentation, is a unique example of early English leather-craft.

Of the ancient priory of Aidan and Cuthbert nothing survives except a few fragments in the collection at the Priory Museum. These we examined the following day when the rain, for a brief time, abated.

The Lindisfarne Gospels

For years the teachers on Lindisfarne were noted for their spirituality, their commitment to the Gospel, and their emphasis on the Bible as the only source of truth and doctrine. It was during this halcyon age on Lindisfarne that the famous Lindisfarne gospels were produced. These superbly illuminated manuscripts, now in the British Museum, are the finest artefacts still remaining of the Celtic Church.

The four gospels and two of the epistles were written on 258 pages of vellum. Most of the pages are plain, the main illumination occurring at the beginning of each gospel where there is a page of elaborate, cruciform design, and a page of ornamented text in pure Celtic style. The cruciform pages are completely covered with an interlaced pattern of birds and animals of intricate design.

The gospels remained at Lindisfarne until the island was abandoned in 875. By 883 the manuscripts were at Chester-le-Street. Here Aldred translated the Latin text into the old Northumbrian dialect, thus making these manuscripts the earliest surviving English version of the gospels. Significant, this; centuries before either Wyclif or Tyndale lived, a Northumbrian monk caught their vision that peasant and ploughboy, as well as king and cardinal, should have access to the Scriptures, and that in their own tongue.

After the monks' departure from Lindisfarne in 875 — under attack from Vikings — it seems possible that the Holy Isle was uninhabited for in excess of two centuries. However, since 1082 there has always been a settlement on the island. In 1120 the monks completed their rebuilding of the ruined priory under whose arches we had sheltered the previous day.

As we drove towards the causeway, the entire island suddenly vanished in a veil of saffron. Bumping our way over potholes hidden beneath the floods, windscreen wipers at maximum speed, we had to search for the causeway to beat the tide. Buffy predicted doom and disaster and seemed quite put out when they didn't happen.

We found a road that twisted and turned around giant sand-dunes on the periphery of the island. On either side was seaweed, and a score of gulls from their nests beneath the lip of the turf, wings extended, followed us noisily. At times it was all too easy to imagine that this causeway was twisting and turning its way across the North Sea. At one time Buffy had me almost convinced that it was.

With the tide lapping at our tyres we made it to the mainland, just in time.

Whitby's Abbey

After the drenching rain of Lindisfarne, the clear day at Whitby came as an unexpected gift. All day the sun shone triumphantly, and nowhere could we escape the endless sound of rejoicing water.

Built in a half-basin opened seaward, the little piled-up town of Captain Cook was brimmed on the landward side by a semicircular, green horizon. Beyond and behind the green brim, wind-swept, tree-bare meadows gave way to the North York moors.

The sea was calm and blue in the pincered, circular harbour in the hollow of the basin.

We climbed the 199 steps out of the town to the church on the high cliff.

The ancient abbey

For soaring ecclesiastical architecture, however, we wandered over to the impressive ruins of the ancient abbey. We pored over the ruins of its mighty towers, archways, pillars, many façades complete, save the windows.

In the years since the dissolution of the monasteries in 1539 the great abbey has suffered from more than the lead-robbers who stripped its roofs. The nave fell in a 'great tempest' in 1762, and the south transept from another 'tempest' the year after. Much of the west front collapsed on a terrible night in November 1794 and the central tower fell on 25 June 1830. By comparison with the elements, the German Imperial Fleet which shelled the abbey on 16 December 1914 did minimal damage.

The Abbess Hilda

St. Hilda chose this hideously-exposed site on the east cliff at Whitby in 657.

St. Hilda's monastery was one of those double monasteries of men and women which formed a marked feature of the early Anglo-Saxon Church. It had not long been completed when it was the scene of the Synod of

Whitby in 664. This synod had enormous significance for the religious history of Britain.

What was decided at the Synod of Whitby was far more than the date of Easter. The central issue was which of the two major strains of Christianity represented in Britain should prevail.

On the one hand there was the Celtic Church, first brought from Ireland, and spread from Iona and Lindisfarne to many parts of Britain and Celtic Europe. The faith of the Celtic Church was Bible-based; had a strong emphasis on what would (many centuries later) become known as the 'Reformation doctrine' of Justification by Faith; practised baptism by immersion; and believed in the second coming of Christ.

On the other hand was the Roman Church which assumed its present character following the conversion of the Emperor Constantine and represented a colourful mixture of pre-Christian practices, bowdlerized Scripture, and pious practice.

Right here where we were standing, on the site of Whitby Abbey, the fate of Christianity in Britain was decided. Colman, Bishop of Lindisfarne, was spokesman of the Celtic Church. Wilfred and numerous representatives from Canterbury, were spokesmen for the Roman party.

When the synod was over Abbess Hilda knew that things had gone the way of Rome. The Celtic clergy left Whitby ill-disposed towards the synod's decision, and while the Celtic Church and its distinctive beliefs and practices lingered on for many centuries thereafter, the dominance of the Roman Church in Britain was never again challenged — until the time of Wyclif.

Whitby's hero

But if Whitby's abbey had cast a chill shadow over British Christianity one of those who occupied its cloisters was to cast an illuminating ray of light into the future. And from this illuminating ray of light would ultimately dawn a new day for Christianity in Britain.

The name of Whitby's hero was Caedmon. Right at

the top of the 199 steps that lead from the town to the windy, exposed ridge where the church and the abbey ruins stand there is an imposing cross to his memory.

And rightly so. In the Celtic tradition Caedmon tried to remove the barrier of language that separated the people from the Scriptures. Not for another 700 years would Geoffrey Chaucer begin to write in the vernacular language of England, and John Wyclif begin to translate the Bible into that language. However, in the last half of the seventh century Caedmon endeavoured to tell in his native tongue the story of man's creation, fall and redemption.

It would appear that Caedmon, a humble cowman, arrived on the steps of the abbey one morning in 670. Bede says: 'St. Hilda ordered him to be instructed in sacred history and Caedmon stored up in his memory all that he learned, and like an animal ruminating turned it into such melodious verse that his delightful renderings turned his teachers into his audience.'

Large portions of the Scripture in manuscript on vellum were available at Whitby Abbey. Soon it would appear that Caedmon committed considerable portions of Scripture to memory. Two hundred and twenty-nine pages of Caedmon's Scripture-converted-to-rhyme are extant in the Bodleian Library, Oxford.

The standard of diction and style, as well as the golden phrases of Caedmon's poetry, inspired thousands of his contemporaries, as well as those who lived in after ages. But the really revolutionary aspect of his achievement was that God's 'lively oracles' were no longer encased in Latin, a language known only to a tiny minority.

—o—

A stiff wind began to blow in from the sea bearing strong, salt smells of northern weather. As the car pulled in second gear up the steep hill out of Whitby, Buffy Trumpton sang the praises of the little town.

Somewhere along the A1 south he asked when and how the Roman had replaced the Celtic tradition elsewhere in the British Isles. And then, having asked the question, began to forage in the half-dozen volumes he had brought with him for answers. He discovered that, even before Northumbria surrendered the faith of the Celtic Church at Whitby in 664, southern Ireland had thrown in its lot with the Italian mission (in 632). The north of Ireland was to do so in 695. The death of the Celtic Church in Scotland was more gradual; but began in 717 with the reign of King Nectan. What Buffy persisted in calling 'the surrender' occurred in the west of England in 768. And 777 is generally accepted as the date when Roman Christianity was accepted in Wales.

Buffy's distinctly 'Protestant' interpretation of the demise of the Celtic Church notwithstanding, somewhere south of Sunderland he began to express an interest in the great religious houses of the Roman Church, the impressive ruins of which remained in North Yorkshire.

CHAPTER ELEVEN

ABBEYS IN THE DALES

' "IF ANYONE WANTS to get an impression of what the great Middle Ages monasteries were like, they must visit the Yorkshire Dales," ' read Buffy Trumpton from some tome he'd picked up at the Oxfam shop. ' "And nowhere can religious houses be found in such heart-liftingly beautiful, even idyllic surroundings . . . ." '

When St. Bernard and his monks left Clairvaux for North Yorkshire in 1131 they carried with them glowing accounts of a tranquil heaven-on-earth of unsurpassable beauty.

They were not to be disappointed. Far, far from it.

By now Buffy and I had been away from base continuously for a long period of time. The call of home and family was strong. But, under warm sun and blue skies, it seemed a pity to pass up the Dales. We phoned south to our wives. They both agreed to meet us at Harrogate and to bring with them some supplies we were missing. More enjoyably, they agreed to spend a fortnight in the dales and moors with us.

So joyful was our reunion that for some days we quite forgot ruined abbeys, and simply explored the natural beauties of this enchanted land.

Swaledale, Coverdale, Wensleydale . . . drystone walls climbing the dizzy gradients of imposing hillsides and patchworking the greener pastures of valley bottoms . . . stone barns and lonely farmsteads dotted around, vulnerable in face of the elements . . . twisting lanes with views of iron-jawed crags, stark, almost menacing . . . .

We visited villages and small towns with names like Thwaite, Hawes, Leyburn, Middleham, Coverham and Aysgarth. Crossing the A1 we drove into Thirsk and, against all the odds, succeeded in meeting the world-famous vet-cum-raconteur James Herriot. He autographed a copy of his beautifully-illustrated book *James Herriot's Yorkshire* (published by Michael Joseph). Taking us through its pages he introduced us to the several wonders of his world.

Late evening, three or four days into our stay, we found ourselves at Aysgarth Falls. We watched the peat-brown waters crashing frantically down and knew why Herriot waxed so lyrical about this very special part of England.

As we went in search of an overnight billet the music of the falls remained in our ears. After a good Yorkshire supper in a nearby farm we went to sleep, perchance to dream of the solitude of bare fells, of swollen, tumbling streams, of empty moors and, high above, a curlew calling.

Rievaulx Abbey

It was the curlew's call that finally fractured our slumbers the following morning and gently, gradually, comfortably roused us to wakefulness.

Over breakfast we were to learn that Buffy and his wife had been up and active almost since dawn. They had watched the blanket of summer morning mist that had, at first, covered meadows and streams. Above and through it they had delineated the high profile of the nearby moorland. It is rewarding to rise early in the Dales!

The car packed, we followed Herriot's directions to Sutton Bank, his favourite spot. Soon, having made our way up a series of steep S-bends, we were looking down on the heart-expanding view he had described. It was a land of freedom and high winds, solitude and purity.

'Peace dwells here in the high moorland,' Herriot had told us, 'stealing across the empty miles, breathing from the silence and the tufted grass and the black peaty earth.'

From Sutton Bank we followed the escarpment into wilder, more jagged terrain. Now the crystal air hung with the smells of everything that grew. All was peace. But it was not difficult to envision this wilder country in less accommodating humour . . . . Long treks across uneven land in the sharp of winter midnight to tend some ailing cow . . . streams gushing out of gullies, turning to dangerous torrents . . . a stone barn with rotting beams and gaping draught-holes, with the valley under a clammy blanket of November fog, and an operation to perform on a heifer, hands shaking with the cold . . . helping round up a flock of sheep caught in a snow blizzard on one of those exposed hillsides with nothing to break the fury of the north wind . . . .

Next we came to Helmsley with its castle and clean, light stone buildings, and wide, sunny square. An artefact from the England of the first two Georges intact, as good as new, with shades of earlier times . . . .

From Helmsley we walked the two miles to the terraces above the steep valley which contains the imposing ruins of Rievaulx Abbey.

The late afternoon brightness cooked the smell of hot pollen from the catmint and cow parsley with the strong tang of wood garlic. Tall, weighted weeds swayed to the sound of foraging bees as we made our way between the two Grecian-style temples belonging to the age of eighteenth-century elegance. Between the tangle of tall weeds and tall trees we peered down into the steep valley and had an almost aerial view of Rievaulx's Gothic ruins.

Buffy reminded us of the arrival of the first Cistercians into this verdant valley in 1131. We imagined the site swarming with the 140 monks and 500 lay brothers of Rievaulx's halcyon age. We all but heard the tinkling bells that broke the silence of monkish mornings and echoed round the valley with the proud anthems and thinner, plaintive sounds of plain chants . . . . We thought of the sad years of decline and decay (only twenty-two monks were left at the time of the Dissolution in 1538), and marvelled at the capacity of the mighty ruins to startle the eye and move the emotions.

When St. Bernard had arrived in this valley, chosen a site for the monastery on the banks of the Rye and installed the first abbot, he had intended it as a Cistercian mission centre. Indeed, from Rievaulx, missions were sent out to found Melrose and Warden (1136), Dundrennan (1142) and Revesby (1143). Even looking at what remains of the vast nave of cathedral proportions, it is still possible to catch a glimpse of Bernard's vision. For 400 years Rievaulx was one of the half dozen great mother-houses of the Cistercian abbeys in the British Isles. It gave birth to many daughters. Among them Byland Abbey, in the same valley but on the other side of the Rye. Rievaulx and Byland did not have to rely on the waters of the Rye. The water supply for both great houses came from the springs on the hillsides.

As we followed the Rye back towards Sutton Bank we could all but hear the chant of the monks echoing among the heather-clad hills.

Fountains Abbey

Next day we followed the route of the monks who found Rievaulx too 'worldly' and went in search of a purer paradise . . . .

Rievaulx, Helmsley, Thirsk and Sutton Bank are technically in the North York Moors. Our forty-mile drive to Fountains Abbey took us across the A1 and into the Dales. By now we were beginning to realize the practical problems of using Buffy's OS maps. It takes four OS maps to cover the area of the moors and dales of North Yorkshire. We stopped at Ripon to enjoy its impressive twelfth-century cathedral and then, in the town, made a conscious search for a more useful map. We struck gold. *The Tourist Map of the Yorkshire Dales* was to prove infinitely more convenient than the OS maps (and is a fraction of their cost).

We had learned enough from Herriot, Herriot's book and sundry other sources to realize that there was enough in Wharfedale alone to occupy us for at least a week. Though there were plenty of bed-and-breakfast establishments around, Mrs. Buffy had a strong penchant for self-catering. Since we were suffering from a certain anaemia of the exchequer, we readily fell in with her idea. We chose Grassington as our Wharfedale base and booked a little self-catering flat over a cafe in the cobble-stoned centre of the village. This was to be an excellent base for our hikes in Wharfedale and neighbouring dales.

By contrast with hiking country elsewhere, the walks in the Dales were well signposted and clearly marked with stoutly-built stiles over the dry-stone walls. And so bowled over was Buffy by the delectability and newness of it all, that he forgot to grumble about his sore feet.

Fountains Abbey, the Abbey of St. Mary de Fontanis, is accessible from the Ripon-Pateley Bridge Road. The bleakness of the early winters during which those monks from Rievaulx cowered under rocky outcrops by night and shivered in the icy winds as they built with the masons by day was impossible to imagine. But what they built in this valley of springs, they built well. So much of it remains that the imagination requires little prompting and it is easy to accept its claim to have been one of the largest religious houses in Christendom.

For four centuries Fountains was alive as a centre of piety and learning. It was a medieval showpiece, a place of pilgrimage. And so it remained. Visitors numbering six figures annually come to look at Fountains. Some gaze up at the abrupt end of a stone staircase — and imagine sleepy monks descending at the summons of the bell to matins. Those with an architectural bent appreciate that the transept at the east end of the church, a lofty rectangular tower, and the vaulted undercroft of the cellarer's range are among outstanding features of their kind. For others the grey arches and buttresses are but an unforgettable picture frame for the memory of a drowsy afternoon on the spacious lawns and among the formal gardens.

Here is the best artefact of the reforming Cistercian current set in motion by the dynamo Abbot of Clairvaux, St. Bernard.

At the time of the dissolution of the monasteries under Henry VIII, William Thirsk was abbot. Thirsk's ill-advised involvement in the Pilgrimage of Grace — one of the two risings against Henry's dissolution policy — led to a scandal being attached to Fountains in its final years. The King's two commissioners were told to grasp every rank shred of rumour to justify dissolution. No one — least of all the King who promised him a generous pension — believed that the abbot kept whores, or was guilty of theft or sacrilege, or that he was a 'miserable idiot'. Nevertheless, government policy required that such accusations be made. It also required that Thirsk, among the best abbots of his period, should be declared guilty of treason and hanged at Tyburn.

The abbey's annual revenue of £1,000, plus £700-worth of plate, ornaments and vestments, together with assets including 1,976 horned cattle, 1,146 sheep, 86 horses and 79 pigs were divided among sundry royal favourites.

Time and aristocratic protection have been kind to Fountains. Even after Dissolution the site was passed from one heritage-conscious, land-owning family to another. As the centuries passed, the partially-ruined abbey became surrounded by vast formal gardens with great lakes and waterfalls absorbing the water from the River Skell and the springs (fountains) which had given the abbey its name. All the landscaping and the waterways are preserved intact. There is a full day's hiking and viewing around the forested hills, great gardens and architecture at Fountains.

Bolton Priory

One day we followed the Wharfe to Bolton Priory. Summer hung over river and meadows. Clouds of midges tingled about the face. We used the stepping stones to cross the river to the priory.

Half the ancient building is in ruins; the other half is still in use as a church. The priory was founded in 1151. The nave built by the Augustinian canons is the part now used as the parish church, while the east end of the monastic house of worship is the ruined skeleton.

We entered to thank God for the blessings of His great creation and, while in prayer, heard the sound of distant plainsong. Coming from the direction of the priory ruins the sound was apt to shove the imagination into overdrive. However, eventually we agreed that it came from some out-of-sight loud-speakers . . . .

Jervaulx Abbey

One remaining religious house in the Dales is deserving of a visit: the Cistercian abbey ruins at Jervaulx near Middleham. The site is privately owned and, though the ground plan of the ancient abbey can be seen well enough, the shrubs, trees and gardens have been allowed to overgrow the ancient stones. The best feature is the wall of the monks' dormitory with a fine row of lancet windows high up. The monastery was founded in 1156, and fifteen different masons' marks are still discernable on the building fragments. The destruction of the abbey took place as a result of the involvement of its last abbot in the Pilgrimage of Grace.

—o—

Any exploration of the Yorkshire moors and dales must, of necessity, take in God's other great cathedral, the open air.

Among the places not to be missed are Wensleydale and Castle Bolton from whence Mary Queen of Scots made her attempted escape. There is a cluster of villages — among them Muker, Reeth and Askrigg — which must be visited, even if only upon the grounds that they are among the most beautiful in England.

The morning we crossed the Buttertubs Pass to reach them is etched upon the memory. Back in Grassington the day had promised well but, as we descended on Hawes, the light changed. Clouds — giant black butts overflowing with thousands of gallons of water — were being shunted by the winds over the roof of Yorkshire. As we traversed Swaledale the grey curtain of rain moved swiftly along the dale, west to east, a swaying, gently undulating curtain, immensely tall and hissing. It met us like a vast, all-enveloping sheet of cold canvas.

—o—

On our final morning in the Dales, Mrs. Buffy came leaping towards me, like Lady Macbeth coming to get first-hand news from the guest room. 'Are we *really* going home?' she asked excitedly, as if she couldn't quite believe it.

I understood exactly what she meant. After long weeks in which her relationship with her husband had taken the form of postcards and short letters written in Buffy's clipped, breezy style, she wanted him home for a while, back in the West One postal district.

Several hours later I was decanting the Trumptons outside the Regency block that contained their mansion flat. 'Fantastic experience, eh?' said Buffy. 'But after all those weeks of fresh air and history, it's good to touch base.' Then, turning to his wife; 'Lunch at the Savoy, old girl? Then dinner at my club, what?'

CHAPTER TWELVE

FROM 'HAIL MARY' TO 'AMAZING GRACE'

'I S'POSE,' SAID Buffy Trumpton on a calm, clear August day, 'that a card-carrying Evangelical like you would not even *consider* taking in Walsingham. Too "Hail Mary", not enough "Amazing Grace" for you, eh?'

'Strike a bargain,' I said. 'We'll take in Walsingham, if *you* can stomach Bunyan and Newton "Amazing Grace" country.'

'No problem,' riposted Buffy. 'Stout fellow, John Newton. Helped Wilberforce get rid of slavery.' And then, after a pause; 'No long walks, what?'

'Not in "Amazing Grace" country,' said I. 'But they used to pilgrimage to Walsingham from all points of the compass in their bare feet . . . .'

Walsingham: a Shrine before Becket

All of which explains how we came to be rollicking through the restful Fenlands towards north Norfolk one summer Sunday. Anita came along for the ride, adding her usual spice and verve.

Bright red poppies were everywhere, covering the banks and striping the fields. But there was field after field of gentle, blue flowers: flax.

In no hurry and having set off early we took in a butterfly farm, an orchid centre and a swift look at Sandringham before we reached the spot intended. And even then, still full of the memories of Walsingham, we were able to take in Cromer, Wells-Next-the-Sea and Hunstanton before dark.

But Walsingham, it must be said, was something of a revelation.

It was in the twilight of Edward the Confessor's Saxon England that the vision occurred. In 1061, to be precise. Richeldis, a Saxon lady with a Norman husband, claimed to have been instructed by the Virgin Mary to build a 'Holy House' patterned on the Nazareth home of Jesus, and to have had this home 'revealed' to her. She built the 'Holy House', it would appear, with Papal approval. Hence, more than a century before Becket's murder, the devout pilgrimaged to Walsingham from all directions. The most favoured one was the 'Walsingham Way' from London. As Buffy was quick to point out, it was at the Slipper Chapel that pilgrims left behind their footwear, walking only the last mile and a quarter barefoot.

In 1130 the Augustinian Canons established a priory near the site of Richeldis' rude Saxon construction. After Henry III's patronage of Richeldis' shrine every English monarch up to and including Henry VIII visited Walsingham.

Parts of the village look sixteenth-century. It would be worth a visit if the Saxon lady had never dreamed about Mary. All major branches of Christianity have a shrine there. The Anglican Shrine of Our Lady claims to cover the spot where the Saxon structure stood. It was packed with pilgrims in prayer. Only a few showed interest in the holy water being dispensed from a well. There was a 'fragment of the true cross' in a glass cabinet, but no one was falling for that one.

Through a stout medieval gatehouse, wedged between the high street shops, we entered the grounds of the priory. The 1538 dissolution left enough behind to fire the imagination and, should the imagination prove sluggish, booklets were on sale with sketches of the grand pre-Reformation structure. Around the endless grounds, fringed by woodland extending out to the dimplement of

Norfolk hills, were nature walks and rivers being enjoyed by children.

When we left Buffy behind in the village, coaches were decanting hundreds of pilgrims, and the narrow streets were becoming thronged, black-robed priests darting purposefully in and around like sheepdogs.

We drove the one-and-a-quarter miles to the Catholic establishment, saw the Slipper Chapel, the vast, modern Church of Reconciliation, and the great gardens surrounded by wooden crosses where mass can be said outdoors. We were driving back to the village when we were stopped by the police and told that we might have to wait an hour.

Getting out of the car and walking to a junction we saw the one-and-a-quarter-mile road out of Walsingham to the Slipper Chapel, hedge to hedge with chanting, banner-carrying Catholics. We read the banners and found that the thousands of pilgrims grouped around their priests had come from all parts of Europe. A few walked barefoot. When the last had gone by and we were back in the car we noticed that there were two stragglers. Buffy was engaged in animated argument with a priest. Both had their shoes on.

John Bunyan country

The day we drove down into Bedfordshire was one of those quiet, calm, restful sunny days that occur only rarely. Before homing in on Elstow, where Bunyan (1628-88) was born, I drove slowly around the surrounding countryside. Here Bunyan the tinker, in the days before he achieved celebrity as a preacher, shouldering his portable anvil (still in the Bunyan Museum, Bedford) walked from village to village plying his trade.

'Do you realize we've just passed through the Valley of the Shadow?' I asked Buffy. 'And that around the next bend is the Enchanted Land? And that, a mile or so back, we passed the place "somewhat ascending" where Christian found the cross?'

'I'm fogged,' said Buffy. 'Give me some footnotes.'

I readily obliged. Not only had I been boning up on *Pilgrim's Progress*, but had even dipped into a detailed exposition of it. Here I had learned that, from Bunyan's vivid descriptions of the places through which Christian passed on his way between the City of Destruction and the Celestial City, could be recognized actual places in the Bedfordshire countryside through which he regularly walked in pursuance of his trade. Thus informed, Buffy had no difficulty in identifying a number of the other sites, more or less unchanged since the seventeenth century.

We parked the car near Elstow church which contains the record of Bunyan's christening and where he felt his first soul-stirrings. The cottage where Bunyan lived with his wife and family has long since disappeared. Nevertheless, it is possible to get an atmosphere of old Elstow. There are still many timbered buildings from Bunyan's time and, in the centre of the green, there is the restored Moot Hall which contains the Bunyan Museum.

Bedford was a very pleasant surprise. The River Ouse winds through the centre of this beautiful city. On either side of the river is landscaped parkland and an embankment walkway. On the river itself there were scores of people 'messing about in boats'.

The Bunyan Meeting on Mill Street was a source of tremendous fascination. After being stationed at Newport Pagnell as one of Cromwell's soldiers, Bunyan returned to Bedford at the finish of the civil wars. In 1650 he was one of a group of twelve who, under John Gifford, had founded this congregation. However, during the years of religious freedom between 1653 and 1660, he had worshipped at St. John's church on the other side of the river, still with Gifford as his pastor. His own preaching had begun in 1657 and his troubles commenced in 1660 with the restoration of the Stuarts. From 1660 to 1672 he was imprisoned. In Bedford's shopping centre, outside Principles, we saw a stone slab in the pavement marking the position of Bedford's infamous gaol. A quarter of a mile away, at a junction of roads, there is an impressive statue of Bunyan with scenes from *Pilgrim's Progress* carved around its plinth.

Bunyan's release from prison had come as a result of Charles II's Declaration of Indulgence. As a result of the new found — but short lived — freedom of religion, the congregation of which Bunyan was pastor began meeting in a barn before building commenced on the present structure. Bunyan was pastor from 1672 until his death in 1688, except for a short intermission for his second period of imprisonment.

The stained glass windows of the Bunyan Meeting represent scenes from *Pilgrim's Progress* (first issued in 1678), one of Bunyan's many published works. As a communion table the chapel still uses a table originally removed from St. John's church to the barn where the (illegal) congregation had met.

Behind the Bunyan Meeting is another Bunyan Museum, this one containing, in addition to Bunyan memorabilia, 160 editions of *Pilgrim's Progress* in many languages.

John Newton's Olney

From Bedford it was but a short drive into Buckinghamshire and to the Olney of hymn writers John Newton (1725-1807) and William Cowper (1731-1800).

The house Newton and his family shared with Cowper has been preserved as the Newton and Cowper Museum and is situated in the main square of the picturesque village. Here the two hymn writers produced *The Olney Hymns* and here Newton struggled with Cowper's periodic bouts of depression.

Not overly interested in hymns and hymn writers, it was the conversion story of John Newton that Buffy was eager to follow up. Newton, he knew, had supplied MP William Wilberforce with much evidence and many artefacts which had been used in his fifty-three-year campaign to abolish, first, the slave trade (1807) and, second, slavery itself (1833). Many of the artefacts of slavery scattered around Newton's house are reminiscent of those to be found in the Georgian house once occupied by William Wilberforce in old Hull. Without doubt the conversion story of John Newton is one of the most remarkable of all time. The story of his involvement as a sea captain in the infamous Middle Passage of the slave trade has been told many times. That Newton was, for a number of years, virtually enslaved himself (in West Africa) is less widely known.

A storm at sea was the occasion rather than the cause of the beginning of Newton's conversion. However, a number of years passed before the slave captain honoured the resolves he made in the storm. In Liverpool he committed his life to Jesus Christ and commenced training for the Anglican ministry. The church he pastored in Olney has a scenic position not far from one of the most beautiful stretches of the River Ouse.

Inside the church is the original pulpit from which John Newton preached. In the churchyard, after diligent search, we found Newton's tomb crammed up against the perimeter wall. Buffy found it and read out the inscription:

'John Newton, Clerk
ONCE AN INFIDEL AND LIBERTINE
A SERVANT OF SLAVES IN AFRICA WAS
BY THE RICH MERCY OF OUR
LORD AND SAVIOUR JESUS CHRIST
PRESERVED, RESTORED, PARDONED
AND APPOINTED TO PREACH THE FAITH HE
HAD LONG LABOURED TO DESTROY.'

Newton's other spiritual testimony is to be found in, perhaps, the greatest of his hymns: Amazing Grace. Buffy sought to recite the words as we stood quietly by the tomb. He made it to the finish, but there were tears in his voice.

To improve the poignant moment I took from my

pocket a copy of *Pilgrim's Progress* and read John Bunyan's wonderful account of Christian's conversion:

'He ran thus till he came to a place somewhat ascending; and upon that place stood a Cross, and a little below . . . a Sepulchre. So I saw in my dream, that just as Christian came up with the Cross, his burden loosed from off his shoulders, and fell from off his back, and began to tumble, and so continued to do, till it came to the mouth of the Sepulchre, where it fell in, and I saw it no more.

'Then was Christian glad and lightsome, and said, with a merry heart, He hath given me rest by His sorrow, and life by His death . . . .'

CHAPTER THIRTEEN

WESLEY COUNTRY

BUFFY TRUMPTON HAD not exactly gone over the top in his
enthusiasm for Wesley's 'Great Awakening' when we had
visited Cornwall. But exposure to Bunyan and Newton
country had rendered him more susceptible to evangelical
influences. Nevertheless it took the promise of Oxford to
persuade him to accompany me on the Wesley trail.

Epworth

What better place to start than Epworth where
England's great apostle was born in 1703? Today we
might think of Epworth as 'just off the M180, ten miles
from the Humber Bridge'. Back in 1703, however, it was
the largest of a small clutch of villages on the Isle of
Axholme, a hard-core amid miles of marshy land and, in
the worst of the winter, accessible only by boat.

As we decanted at Epworth, Buffy had clearly decided
to humour me. Grabbing the Rolle, he insisted on photo-
graphing me in preaching pose by the market cross and
standing on the tomb of the Revd Samuel Wesley, from
which vantage points John preached after being excluded
from preaching in his late father's church.

The relatively spacious present-day rectory is the one
built for the large Wesley family after the original rectory had been burned down. The burning of the old
thatched rectory had taken place when John was 5, and
the trauma of the last-minute rescue had etched itself
upon his memory to the extent that he appropriated the

105

text 'a brand plucked from the burning' (Zechariah 3:2) as his own.

In the couple of hours we spent exploring the 'new' rectory, we caught some of the ambience in which John and his siblings were taught by the formidable Susanna. Salvation, they learned, was 'by universal obedience, by keeping all the commandments of God' in the details of which they were 'diligently instructed' (Wesley's *Journal*).

Each ancient room with its authentic furniture was like a time capsule.

We gazed at John's great Bible. Then at the 'lectern' specially fashioned to fit over the horse's neck so that John could read as he rode. Travelling 6,000 miles or more a year and preaching up to a dozen times a day, we imagined him reading as his horse trotted along the rutted tracks that passed for roads in eighteenth-century England.

From some of the etchings we caught a picture of his travels to Tyneside where, arriving at 5am, he preached for an hour to the coal miners emerging from the night shift — and received a hearing! We imagined him at Wednesbury, the town in uproar, a mob of local toughs hot on his trail. Until, that is, he was rescued single-handedly by the prize fighter who subsequently became a leading Methodist preacher!

Tyneside, West Yorkshire, London, Bristol and Cornwall: these were the population centres between which Wesley was constantly on the move.

Oxford

On our journey to Oxford we passed by Lincoln Castle where old Samuel Wesley was imprisoned for debt during the childhood of John.

But it was as the Oxford skyline hove into view that Buffy really became ecstatic (almost). Nor was his (almost) ecstasy in any way diminished by the fact that Matthew Arnold's 'sweet city with her dreaming spires' was juddered through by juggernauts!

Getting shot of the car as soon as possible we aimed

for Magdalen Bridge and looked over the green sward towards Magdalen's Tower, Buffy chanting the while, 'We twa hae run about the braes, and pu'd the gowans fine . . . '.

Before homing in on Lincoln College — Wesley's college — we decided on a quick jaunt around the old place for sentiment's sake.

Outside each college was a glittering forest of parked bicycles, Balliol seemingly having the most. Near Balliol was the monument to Archbishop Thomas Cranmer and Bishops Latimer and Ridley. These Cambridge-educated scholars were burned on that spot in 1555 by Mary I for their Protestant beliefs. At the time Balliol's door was singed by the fire; and the singed door remains. There is an air of greatness about Christ Church; its *alumni* include eighteen prime ministers. The earliest organized college was Merton founded in 1262 by Walter de Merton, Lord Chancellor of England.

Only when we escaped from the noisy streets, through the archways, past eagle-eyed porters, were we able to enjoy the Oxford of the green, tree-shaded quadrangles. Once again we soaked up the atmosphere of Trinity, Jesus, Queen's and Hertford colleges. We admired the varied architectural styles around Radcliffe Square, including the circular Radcliffe Camera.

Finally we savoured Lincoln College where John and Charles Wesley founded a movement that redirected a nation's history by taking the Gospel to the people.

But it should not be forgotten that Wesley was an undergraduate at Christ Church before becoming a fellow of Lincoln College. Here a combination of Epworth-legalism and a degree of passion totally absent from the established church of his day, led John Wesley to found the Holy Club. This club, whose members were nick-named 'Methodists', included John's younger brother Charles and the later-to-be-famous George Whitfield. All agreed that the nation needed revival.

The failure of Wesley's evangelism in America, his exposure to the Moravians with their joy and their justification, the misery resulting from the failure of his strivings to renounce evil and cultivate virtue, and the conversion (and resultant greater effectiveness) of George Whitfield, led Wesley consciously to search for revival in his own experience. And that vital revival was to take place in London.

London and Bristol

For a man who rarely, from choice, went north of Watford, and believed, from conviction, that the West One postal district contained every necessity for life, Buffy's knowledge of London was deplorably deficient. Had it been otherwise, on the occasion of our search for Wesley in London, he could have saved himself a long and arduous trek.

It was another blisteringly hot day when we walked up the City Road towards Wesley's chapel and Wesley's house. Our walk had begun at Kings Cross, and Buffy was unprepared for the length of the walk and for the fact that it was mainly uphill.

In 1739 Wesley realized the need for a headquarters building from which to co-ordinate his rapidly-growing movement. He originally bought a disused foundry. It cost £115, and a further £800 to be made suitable for a meeting room and living quarters. The foundry served the Methodist movement for forty years. At the end of this period, despite repeated repairs, it was quite clearly falling apart. It was then that the decision was taken to buy the plot on the City Road just opposite to the Bunhill Fields where the great dissenters were buried. On 21 April 1777 Wesley laid the foundation stone of the City Road Chapel.

As we explored the chapel and the museum attached to it we thought there was an unmistakable eighteenth-century 'feel'. We experienced the same 'feel' when we explored John Wesley's four-storey house immediately next to the chapel. Having read a moving account of Wesley's death-bed scene, Buffy was slightly unnerved when we entered the small bedroom to see the bed and furnishings just as they had been at the time of the great man's demise in 1791.

Wesley's tomb is behind the City Road chapel and overlooked by a semicircle of plate glass reaching skywards. Having paid our respects we crossed the City Road opposite and walked through Bunhill Fields. John Bunyan's tomb was the first to take our attention.

From Bunhill Fields we made our way to St. Paul's by way of Aldersgate Street. As we walked along, almost by accident, we noticed an engraved slab on a vast modern building. It announced that here was the probable site of John Wesley's conversion in 1738.

Wesley had, it will be recalled, been conscious of a need for a revival in his own experience before he could lead a nation in revival. His exposure to the Moravians, in particular, prepared him for his experience at Aldersgate Street on 21 May 1738. That evening he had left his brother Charles at the lodgings they shared. At Aldersgate Street someone was reading Luther's preface to his *Epistle to the Romans*. Wesley was to write in his *Journal* that he felt his 'heart strangely warmed'. 'I felt I did trust in Christ, Christ alone for salvation; and an assurance was given me that He had taken away *my* sins, even *mine*, and saved *me* from law of sin and death.'

In a state of elation John Wesley returned, with his friends, to the lodgings he shared with Charles. Charles had spent the evening composing a new hymn to a Moravian tune they both knew. The group gathered around the harpsichord and sang the hymn reading the words over Charles's shoulder. They could hardly have been more appropriate for John's experience:

> 'And can it be that I should gain
> An interest in the Saviour's blood!
> Died He for me, who caused His pain?
> For me, who Him to death pursued?
> Amazing love! How can it be?
> That thou my God shouldst die for me?'

Wesley was now free of 'the method' he had taught in

Oxford which, in turn, had been based on the legalism he had learned at his mother's knee. Now he was free to lead a nation in revival.

From London we headed west to Bristol, as Wesley must have done very many times. The rain had come. We were in a car on the M4; Wesley would have been on horseback, exposed to the elements, as well as to uncertain, unmade-up roads.

Our visits to the Wesley sites in Bristol were wedged in between speaking commitments and were therefore, perforce, brief.

Awkwardly imprisoned in a maze of shopping precincts, we found the home of Charles Wesley, author of some 6,000 hymns. Outside his home was his statue.

Behind Charles Wesley's house, but accessible from quite a different precinct, was the old Wesleyan Centre in Bristol, the New Room. To enter the New Room we passed the statue of John Wesley on horseback.

Coming from the New Room was the sound of singing. For the third time that year we were to gatecrash a meeting organized to commemorate the bicentenary of Wesley's death. And, appropriately, their commemoration was taking the form of a celebration of the lives of the Wesley brothers. John, we were told, had written many of the hymns subsequently attributed to Charles. Regardless of author, however, these hymns were without question written to be sung and the tunes vigorous.

CHAPTER FOURTEEN

AUTUMN SUNSHINE:
In search of the English Bible

SUMMER WAS STILL hanging on in the fields as we nosed north. The golden crops had given way to golden stubble as if to make room for autumn. But it declined to come. Hence it was in opulent warmth, though late September, that we hove to at Barnard Castle.

John Wyclif

We were in search of John Wyclif and on the trail of the English Bible. But bees still buzzed in the cow parsley, and we could not bring to our quest any sense of urgency.

From the castle we looked down at the waltzing, waters of the Tees. Buffy was smiling his sunny smile and looking like a boy about to be taken to the circus. It was that kind of day. He had already sauntered round the town and chatted to anyone who felt like chatting. At length, he decided it was time to pass on what he had learned to me. 'All the books say Wyclif was born at Barnard Castle circa 1320, but nobody's heard of him here! Might at least have stuck a statue in the High Street! Met a chap who thought Wyclif was a town five miles down the road. As pronounced a fathead as ever broke biscuit!' he said more in languor than anger.

'Might be worth dragging out your OS map,' I suggested.

'Pippin of an idea,' responded Buffy, and unravelled

his map in time for the lively wind that had begun to blow down from the hills of County Durham to start taking an interest in it.

Only when we had the map securely anchored to the car bonnet with hefty volumes was Buffy able to bring his magnifying glass to bear on it. After some minutes he emitted a characteristic yodel.

Wyclif, it appeared, was not so much 'a town five miles down the road', but the tiniest of hamlets in the back of beyond clinging to the steep banks of the Tees. We decided to leave it till morning.

The maze of roads and tracks that took us to Wyclif had grass growing through the middle of them. Before discovering the hamlet we drove across a suspension bridge home-made with planks, the River Tees rushing noisily far below. There was a curious, flat-roofed church with a font so ancient that it predated the hamlet's most famous son. There was also a curious arrangement of bells. Nearby was an ancient manor house built, we discovered, on the site of an even more ancient manor house which had once been home to the man who was first to translate the Bible into English.

John of Wyclif, son of the lord of the manor, had left home at 14 and been admitted to Balliol College, Oxford. Later he was to become Master of his college although, at the same time, being priest in turn at Fillingham, Lincolnshire, and Lutterworth, Leicestershire.

Having discovered John Wyclif's birthplace, we made for Scotch Corner and, from thence, to Richmond Castle. Here had lived John of Gaunt, the royal protector of 'the Morning Star of the Reformation'. Heading south we took in Fillingham — not far from Epworth — and found a record of Wyclif's pastorate, before heading for Lutterworth.

It was at Lutterworth, we discovered, that Wyclif is best remembered. With some reverence we were conducted around the church where, for some years, this man-before-his-time thundered his reforming sermons while fending off papal bulls.

Using the facilities of Oxford as well as the assistance of other Oxford scholars like Nicholas Hereford, Wyclif had managed to produce the first 'Wycliffite' Bible by the time of his death in 1384. Wyclif and his colleagues had translated Jerome's 1,000-year-old Latin Vulgate into English.

The second and better known 'Wycliffite' Bible made its appearance four years after Wyclif's death and, almost certainly, represents a scholarly revision by Wyclif's friend John Purvey of the first translation. One hundred and seventy hand-written copies of this version are still extant.

Wyclif's Bibles continued to be copied throughout the fifteenth century, and Wyclif's reforming views continued to be preached by his 'Lollards'. The 'heresy' of Wyclif, as well as his English Bibles, combined with the influence of Lutheranism to spark the English Reformation. Until the eve of the Reformation Lollards and Lollard Bibles were still being burned in London and Oxford.

William Tyndale

More than a century after Wyclif's death his mantle fell on the shoulders of William Tyndale. Tyndale inherited the vision to take the Bible to the people. He studied at both Oxford and Cambridge and first surfaced on the stage of history as tutor to the children of Sir John Walsh, the squire of Little Sodbury, a village in his native Gloucestershire.

Before setting out for the south-west we put in at home base to recharge our toothbrushes. As we repacked the Peugeot the sky was brilliant-blue and clear of clouds. Though we were into October the daytime temperatures had not dropped below 70 degrees Fahrenheit for days. It was impossible to think of sheeting rain and puddled terrain. So in went short-sleeved shirts and sandals. Boots and anoraks were left at home.

Twenty-four hours later the Peugeot was rollicking drunkenly down the lanes of the Chalford Valley. The whole sky opened up and poured oceans of rain into those steep, deep, dangerously-bending lanes, and huge volumes of ferocious water rushed down far faster than the Peugeot.

Before we reached Little Sodbury we had learned a vital lesson: boots and waterproof clobber are essential for hiking, regardless of immediate weather outlook.

As we set out to explore the little town the rain abated and the sun emerged. Now we saw the meaning of it all. There is a depth of lush green in the valleys of Gloucestershire. How could the valley walls and bottoms be so rich without heaven's copious outpourings?

But, having taught us a lesson, Gloucestershire was now kind. The verdant meadows and the emerald sweep of the narrow, tree-stuffed valleys were bathed in warming, beaming sunshine. Autumn had still to foreclose, and winter was far away.

In the tree-clad slopes there was much to remind us of the storied past of this county of wealth and wool. The force of the hillside streams, and the surging flow of the valley-bottom rivers had once driven great wooden waterwheels. In turn *they* had driven the wool-based economy of the Middle Ages. Then Gloucester and Stroud and Cirencester had stood taller yet among the cities of England.

It was in the manor house at Little Sodbury that Tyndale announced his intention of translating the Bible out of the original Hebrew and Greek so that even the plough-boy could read it.

After an anti-papal speech at dinner he was obliged to flee on foot to London. There he expected to secure the patronage of the bishop, Cuthbert Tunstall.

But Tunstall proved a disappointment. Tyndale went into hiding at Barking. Here, in the home of Humphrey Monmouth, a merchant, he began his work of translation.

Tunstall, now his arch enemy, made England too hot for him. Between 1523 and his martyrdom in 1536 Tyndale kept on the move between Hamburg, Wittenberg, Cologne, Worms and Antwerp, constantly pursued by agents eager to prevent his publication of an English Bible and do him to death.

Nevertheless, from Worms, Tyndale New Testaments began to be smuggled into England.

In England, Tyndale's friends were burned at Smithfield, and his Bibles near St. Paul's. Nevertheless, with the assistance of Miles Coverdale, Tyndale translated the Old Testament and revised his translation of the New before Imperial agents finally caught up with him and he was strangled, then burned at Vilvorde Castle in the Netherlands.

Tyndale's martyrdom did nothing to quench demand for his Bibles. Within months of his death an English Bible, substantially Tyndale's work, made its semi-authorized appearance. And, according to the experts, when the King James Bible was published in 1611 it gave evidence that the translators had leaned heavily on the work done by Tyndale in the 1520s and 30s.

The Wales of Mary Jones

From Gloucestershire we crossed the border into Wales in pursuit of the story of a remarkable girl who, centuries after Wyclif and Tyndale, was to help their dream to become reality. They had made the Bible available in the vernacular. But it was priced out of the pockets of the ordinary man and woman.

All that changed as a result of the formation of the Bible Society. And the Bible Society was founded as a direct result of the story of Mary Jones who walked the Word to the world.

The Mary Jones story was a new one on Buffy. And, as the Peugeot rattled its way over the mountains of central Wales, he gave tongue to many a doubt about our expedition. His doubts were intensified by the knowledge that the expedition would involve a long hike, the longest we had undertaken since the Pilgrim Way. I wanted to walk the twenty-six miles Mary had walked to Bala in search of her Bible.

An autumn pallor began to mask the watery sun,

lending more substance to Buffy's doubts. And each day the sun seemed to be fighting a losing battle and to emerge a little later through the mists.

At length we found the roofless cottage containing the stone monument that marked it as Mary's birthplace. Nearby were the southern slopes of the Cader Idris and the gable end of Tyn-y-Ddol.

In that cottage, in late eighteenth-century Wales, Mary had dreamed the impossible dream of owning a Bible in her own language. Her father was a weaver and his home the factory. Mary helped around the home and only learned to read as a result of the 'circulating schools' scheme whereby a teacher would stay in a particular area long enough to teach the local children to read. Her textbook: the Bible in Welsh.

From her Welsh chapel Mary received an inextinguishable passion for the Scriptures. This passion was fired further when she visited a nearby village, Abergynolwyn, and was permitted access to a Welsh Bible, translated by William Morgan some 200 years previously.

From that exposure to the Bible she used every spare moment to work, scratch and save enough money to buy her own Bible. It took her six years to raise the required sum. And, even then, this was only made possible by the fact that SPCK had published a (relatively) low-cost Welsh Bible.

The news of this low-cost Bible filtered through to Mary's home and, at the age of 16, she set out to walk the twenty-six miles to Bala to buy her Bible.

In my efforts to induce Buffy to undertake Mary's twenty-six-mile trek I had to use every device in the book. The one that worked was an impassioned telling of Mary's story. As I came to the punch line Buffy was just finishing his beans on toast. Suddenly he stood up. 'I'll do it! I'll do it instanter! Come on! Encourage me with word and gesture!'

And so, suitably attired, we were off around the slopes of Cader Idris.

Buffy was going good. As we trudged by the Tal-y-

Llyn Lake, clouds covering the mountain tops, he was filled with determination and bathed in sweat.

We took the A487 over the pass and headed down towards Dolgellau. Keeping clear of the town we followed the river valley of the Afon Dyfrdwy in a north-easterly direction until it flowed into Lake Bala.

We stumbled into Bala just after 5pm with a tremendous sense of achievement. Mary Jones must have had much the same feeling. But her feeling of achievement would have been at least part eclipsed by one of anticipation. And it was this sense of anticipation that was in for a cruel disappointment.

At Bala they had sold out of SPCK Bibles! She had come too late and the tears flowed freely. Only when she told her story to Thomas Charles did anyone realize that her trek had come at the end of long years of self-denial and deserved to be rewarded. Charles took a Bible with a 'reserved' sign on it — and let Mary have it. She had never been happier.

This same Thomas Charles was to attend a meeting of the Religious Tract Society in London in 1802. It was an interdenominational society set up to satisfy the great need for Welsh Bibles. In this forum he told Mary's story and all were moved. Joseph Hughes realized, more than any other, the implications of the story: a story about a young girl's long struggle to buy a Welsh Bible, was also an argument to make available low-cost Bibles for the ordinary people of all lands. This was to be the aim and purpose of the British and Foreign Bible Society which he helped to found in 1804.

At a suitable hostelry Buffy put his feet up before a roaring coal fire. By the time I left to recover the Peugeot, his face had taken on the colour of a devout tomato.

'Fancy the Pembrokeshire coast path, tomorrow?' I asked before exiting the room at some speed.

CHAPTER FIFTEEN

WALES, AND WINTER COMING ON

NEXT MORNING WHEN the car pulled up outside the Bala hostelry where Buffy had spent the night, I could see his capacious form astride the doorway. He informed me in no uncertain terms that he had hiked enough miles already that year to last a lifetime and that if I thought he was about to add the 200 miles of the Pembrokeshire coast path to the tally then I had, well, and with the best will in the world, another think coming.

After I had given the appropriate assurances, he emerged with his battered suitcase, slung it into the boot and, still giving me a cautious look, belted up beside me. He was immensely relieved when he saw I was heading north. The truth was that, even a week earlier, I had harboured an ambition to walk the Pembrokeshire coast path from Cardigan to Tenby and, hiking to Bala the previous day, I had still not given up on the idea entirely. However, overnight, it was as if summer had drifted into autumn. The maiden-blush roses in the gardens were all shed, washed away in the pouring rain.

Hence we were about to embark on a tour of the ancient Christian sites of Wales — by car.

Christian beginnings in Wales

In the British Heroic Age — the age of Arthur, Ambrosius and Vortigern preserved in song and story — vast numbers of Celts had migrated to Wales in face of the advancing Saxon hordes. And, in migrating, they had brought their distinctive form of Christianity with them. The practices and traditions of the Celtic Church were to hold on longer in Wales than in any other part of the British Isles. The story of seventh-century Wales is a story of the conflict between the Celtic Church and the Roman Order.

But it was not from the East that Christianity first came to Wales. It was from the West; immigration from Patrick's Ireland. Hence Christianity's roots in Wales are in the south and west, the areas settled by the incoming Irish. The first great leader was St. Illtyd — an active Christian from 475 to 535 — who founded a monastery at Llantwit Major near Barry and another on Caldey Island off Tenby. On the heels of St. Illtyd came St. David himself, a contemporary of Columba, who founded the greatest Christian centre in Wales: the monastery at St. David's from which the ancient kingdom of Dyfed was won for Christ.

Mungo and Asaph

Finding ourselves at Bala, we decided to visit the early sites in north Wales first. Accordingly we took the A494 and the A525 to St. Asaph in the beautiful Vale of Clwyd, south of Rhyl.

Here was an area evangelized by Mungo, a missionary who had begun his work on the Clyde. Buffy was not slow to point out the similarity in pronunciation between 'Clyde' and 'Clwyd', no accident, of that he was certain. Mungo's monastery had been at Llanelwy. The site is now covered by St. Asaph's small but beautiful cathedral. The cathedral and the town were named after Mungo's most distinguished disciple.

We left the cathedral to the wail of choir boys in liturgical treble. We took in Bangor Is-y-coed on the River Dee, a sixth-century theological college where Celtic Abbot Dinooth had his celebrated confrontation with Augustine. Thereafter we aimed the car toward Anglesey, stopping over at beautiful Conwy for the night.

Anglesey and the Lleyn Peninsula

After passing over the Menai Bridge it was obvious that autumn had finally foreclosed. The leaves on Anglesey were turning gold and brown. Bright, thin sunshine was burnishing the slate roofs. Wind whistled to the sound of hurrying car tyres softly stuttering over the cobbled streets. Booksellers stood next to their tiny stalls, the warmth of their breath vaporizing in the coldness of the afternoon. The taste of the autumnal air was as fresh as lollipops.

When Seiriol and other Christian missionaries took on Anglesey they were confronting paganism at one of its most important centres. In Buffy's words, 'the place must have been lousy with Druids'. When Seiriol founded his priory at Penmon, on the eastern extremity of the island, he had established a toehold for Christ on the island of the Druids.

Beyond the sands of Red Wharf Bay we came upon Din Lligwy. Here we found evidence of a Celtic settlement occupied in Roman and pre-Roman times. Here too Seiriol and other Christian missionaries had worked. Extensive excavation has taken place in the area of the Christian settlement they established. Stone houses have also been excavated in the vicinity as well as buildings of considerable size indicative that this must have been a centre for local chieftains.

From Anglesey we made for the Lleyn Peninsula. For reasons we never really discovered, accommodation was hard to come by in Criccieth. In the end following a sign through a gateway, we drove the car along a tortuous roadway through thick woodland. Eventually the woodland opened out on to a large expanse of serrated rock where we parked. Here was an enormous T-shaped stone house. We knocked on the door and were told that we could book the older part of the house for a week if we so wished. We indicated that one night would be sufficient and were led to a door in the portion of the house built in 1620. Before entering the house we thought that the self-catering aspect of the arrangement would provide the most difficulties. Upon entry, however, we found that food was the least of our worries. The landlady had beat a hasty retreat, and there was no one to complain to. She had told us that Cromwellian soldiers had been billeted here during the siege of Criccieth Castle. What she had *not* prepared us for was that the house was still in the state in which the Cromwellian soldiers had left it . . . . We found ourselves constantly looking over our shoulders and making determined endeavours to ascertain the source of all noises-off, of which there were more than one would have expected. The 'staircase' was made up of large blocks of stone. The horsehair beds were large, but hard and lumpy. We slept little and left in a hurry in the morning, breakfasting in the main street of Llanystumdwy next door to the dwelling in which David Lloyd George was reared.

The road to Aberdaron was scenic but long. Buffy was tetchy. A walk under warm, autumn sunshine on the expansive sands of Hell's Mouth served to improve his temper a little. But at Aberdaron he expressed the view that the journey had been worthwhile.

In the seventh century, we learned, Aberdaron had been used as a place for lodging pilgrims and as a point of embarkation for Bardsey Island. The religious settlement on the island had been founded by students from Bangor Is-y-coed after a battle in which the King of Northumbria had killed 2,000 Celts, some of them fellow students. In the face of difficulties that we cannot even begin to imagine, the surviving students had transported the 2,000 corpses across north Wales, down the Lleyn Peninsula for burial on Bardsey Island. The battle had taken place in 617 and, as the story of the students became known in the years thereafter, Bardsey Island became an important place of pilgrimage.

As we began to retrace the miles back to Criccieth, Buffy was a touch morose. Until, that is, he recalled that a distant branch of the Trumpton tribe was based at Aberystwyth. Although, by our standards, more than a day's journey away, Buffy insisted that we 'biff on to Abbo' to spend the night. The experience at the early seventeenth-century dwelling outside Criccieth had, he assured me, marked him for life.

He phoned ahead to warn his relatives of our approach. It was minutes after midnight when we came alongside a spacious dwelling lit by lanterns. In the light of the lanterns Buffy had spotted one of his own. Before the car had come to a stop, he leapt out with a whoop and a holler, greeting his long-lost relation as 'Ye old flesh-and-blood'!

Rarely did we enjoy a night's lodging more. At breakfast the following morning we were fed until there was a distinct danger of us going straight back to sleep.

'It's the best breakfast I've ever tasted,' said I.

'You speak absolute sooth!' riposted Buffy.

Before waving us on our way Buffy's esteemed relative showed us around a thirteenth-century church which had been built on the site of a sixth-century Celtic monastery. The church was at Llanbadarn Fawr, on the edge of Aberystwyth. The Celtic foundation had been established by Padarn who had trained at Llantwit Major and who is believed to have brought Christianity to many of the isolated settlements of central Wales.

Llantwit Major

We thanked Buffy's relatives most profoundly for their hospitality. 'A good deed in a naughty world,' quoth Buffy. And, so saying, he fell sound asleep, remaining in a more-or-less comatose state until he caught the distinctive scent of a Little Chef somewhere on the A40 and realized it must be lunchtime.

We reached the object of our journey — Llantwit Major, fifteen miles south-west of Cardiff — at 3.30 in the afternoon. Here Illtyd had founded the first Christian settlement in Wales in the early sixth century. Much of what we know of Illtyd we owe to a manuscript written by one of his disciples, Samson. 'Now this Illtyd,' wrote the scholar, 'was the most learned of all the Britons in his knowledge of the Scriptures, both Old and New Testaments.' From the same source we learn that Illtyd was also responsible for establishing the monastery on Caldey Island, off Tenby. This we were to visit the following day and, in so doing, learn that Samson was its abbot. Samson's writings also attribute to Illtyd the evangelization of Cornwall. It would appear that the saint ended his days preaching the Gospel in Brittany.

Llantwit was a place of much greater importance a millennium ago than it is now. Kings were brought to be buried there. However, John Wesley considered it sufficiently important to preach there in 1777 admiring, as he did so, the various artefacts. The Celtic cross dedicated to Illtyd and Samson is certainly of considerable interest — though of indeterminate age — as are a variety of other stone monuments together with the excavations of the ancient monastic site.

However, perhaps because we were fresher, perhaps because of the sunshine or the scenery, we found the following day's visit to Caldey and Tenby a great deal more enjoyable.

St. David's

The National Trust Book of Long Walks by Adam Nicolson is an indispensable guide to the Pembrokeshire coast path. This 200-mile walk is not for the faint-hearted. But, for all that, exposes the hiker to some of the best scenery in the British Isles and is as fascinating to the geologist as to the historian. A fit, experienced hiker might cover these 200 difficult miles in under two weeks. But there is enough to interest a family including teenagers; though they should allow about twenty days. Judging by the time it took us to cover the six or seven miles from Solva to St. David's, Buffy expressed the view that he could never have completed the journey.

Solva was a source of considerable fascination to both of us. Here the sea sweeps in and around to a large sheltered cove where once square-riggers were built. Now pleasure craft cover the whole of the large inlet.

By his own admission Buffy had begun the journey at Solva feeling like something the Pure Food committee had rejected. Nevertheless, as we looked back to Solva from the vantage point of the headland, morning sunshine descending like an amber shower, his spirits were much improved. For the remainder of the journey the milk of human kindness was sloshing about inside him like the rising tide. Asked whether it was the sight of the (agreed) end to our year-long pilgrimage that had improved his spirits, Buffy replied (in Latin): '*Acu tetigisti.*' ('You have touched the matter with a needle.')

We took our time looking down from the tall cliffs at the mountainous waves bursting in a thunderous explosion of foam against the cliff face, enveloping all in a great white beauty, to pour away again, leaving the rocks below black and teeming.

At last we had reached journey's end: St. David's. It is the most westerly town in Wales and also ranks as Britain's smallest city.

St. David's shares the distinction of being at once a town and a cathedral city with St. Asaph. In no sense does the blue sandstone cathedral dominate St. David's. It nestles in a leafy valley, and only the upper part of its lofty central tower is visible from the town square.

The cathedral was built on the site of a monastery founded by St. David in the sixth century. The greater part of the present-day cathedral dates from the end of the twelfth century. The cathedral shares its tranquil valley with the extensive and deeply-romantic ruins of the medieval Bishop's Palace. Present-day St. David's seems remote. By contrast, from the Celtic period to the High Middle Ages, this town was on the main route to Ireland and, at least from an ecclesiastical standpoint, was a very busy place. In its heyday the palace could have housed all the bishops in Europe.

When we walked to the edge of the small 'city' at the close of the afternoon the silent woods and bushes appeared lavender and the sky was an enamelled green in the east. As we turned in to our billet there was, it appeared, an air of expectation.

Next morning I was awoken by Buffy pummelling on my door. Looking out of the small, latticed window on to Cross Square it was clear that, silently and in darkness, snow had covered everything. All things were now rounded, and different, as by a marvel. Even the air seemed to have been given presence. The boughs of the evergreens around the cathedral drooped low, heavy with their white burden. Above was the clear blue of the sky like a bowl that has been decisively emptied.

We had reached journey's end but, to our surprise, we felt in no hurry to leave this timeless place of pilgrimage, its origin so close to the cradle of Christianity. Here seemed to converge all the themes of an eventful year. St. David's in its long history, has been, at once, a place of monastic retreat and pious pilgrimage, and a place where from the distant mists of time Christ's Gospel of pardon, peace and assurance has been preached. It is a place where Patrick, Columba and David could have encountered Wyclif, Tyndale and Wesley — and found common ground. And even the monks in their retreat would not have found themselves too ill at ease. For the monks of St. David's retreated to advance; communed with God and with the Word in order to ignite their souls and inflame the world.

—o—

My route back to base took in the West One postal district. Buffy's wife, family and an immense amount of provender were somehow crammed into and strapped on to the Peugeot. Buffy and I had decided to round off our year of pilgrimage by bringing our families to celebrate Christmas.

Christmas Eve found us in Lincoln. The steep streets of the old city, bedecked with bunting and coloured lights, were crammed with the annual Christmas fair.

In mid-afternoon we stood beside Brayford Pool and looked up at the great Gothic cathedral high on the hill. For a few moments, between the clouds, a sunburst moving west to east illuminated this massive monument built to the greater glory of God. It was like a symbol and a benediction.

By 4.30 we were atop the hill, there was red in the sky and the air was bruisingly cold. The sound of carols wafted from the great west door.

The crowds were leaving the fair and entering the cathedral through the Exchequer Gate. We all followed on.

Inside the cathedral the pillared gloom was lighted and the atmosphere festive though, in the absence of heating, the body's extremities were ice-wet and stone-cold.

But, among the Scriptures and the carols, we found fresh and warming the story of a Boy born a King, born to die, to rise again, that had inspired the greatest men and the finest deeds in our nation's story. From our year's pilgrimage we felt not only closer to the story, but to the story's central Subject: the Risen Jesus.